Polish Touches

RECIPES AND TRADITIONS
"Polish-American Ways" Revised and Expanded

Polish Eagle Dancers Keri and Peter Bas
Houston, Texas

Penfield Press

On the covers

Front cover: The Lira Singers, shown in authentic costumes from Poland, are part of the Lira Ensemble of Chicago, Illinois, the nation's only professional performing arts company dedicated to Polish music, song, and dance. Artistic director and general manager Lucyna Migala is in front. The company, which also includes a chamber chorus, chamber orchestra, children's chorus, and dancers, is based at Montay College as artists-in-residence.

Back cover: Christmas in Kraków as depicted at the Polish Musem of America in Chicago, Illinois.
Polish Easter eggs (pisanki) from the collection of Rev. Czesław Krysa of Orchard Lake, Michigan.

About the Editors

Jacek Nowakowski is curator of the United States Holocaust Memorial Museum in Washington, D.C., and former curator of the Polish Museum of America in Chicago. With a degree in architecture, Nowakowski came to America in 1981 from Poland. A naturalized American citizen, he lives with his wife, two daughters and a son in Bethesda, Maryland.

Marlene J. Perrin is a writer, editor, and researcher in Iowa City, Iowa. She has a degree in journalism from the University of Iowa.

Credits

Photograph editor: Joan Liffring-Zug.
Graphic design: Esther Feske.
Contributing editors and consultants: Miriam Canter, Kathryn Chadima, Dorothy Crum, Krystyna Gutt, Georgia Heald, Julie McDonald, Harry Oster, Michelle Nagle, John Zug and Joan Liffring-Zug.

Library of Congress catalog card number 95-69795
ISBN 1-57216-016-0

Books by mail postpaid:
Polish Touches, Polish -American Ways, $14.95, two for $25
Polish Proverbs, collected by Joanne Asala with wycinanki by
    Alice Wadowski-Bak, $10.95
Pleasing Polish Recipes (spiral bound), $6.95
Complete catalog of all titles, $2
Penfield Press, 215 Brown Street, Iowa City, Iowa 52245

Contents

Acknowledgments

We thank the recipe contributors and those mentioned in this book. Others who contributed include Edward G. Dykla, national president, Polish Roman Catholic Union of America; Daniel J. Kij, president of the Polish Union of America; Rev. Stanley Milewski and priests and staff, Orchard Lake Schools, Orchard Lake, Michigan; Robb DeWall, Crazy Horse Memorial, Crazy Horse, South Dakota; Tim Kuzma, Polonia Song and Dance Company, Pittsburgh, Pennsylvania; Shirley Ann Galanty, Dearborn Heights, Michigan; Father Gabriel Lorenc of the National Shrine of Our Lady of Częstochowa, Doylestown, Pennsylvania; Mrs. Albin Gorecki, Pennington, New Jersey; Eugene E. Rosypal, executive director, Polish American Congress; the staff of the Polish American Museum, Chicago, Illinois; the staff of the Polish Consulate, Chicago; Ellen Wierzewski, assistant executive director, Copernicus Foundation, Chicago; Jolanta Drake, New Berlin, Wisconsin; Jacquie Allen-Lodico, director, Niagara Council of the Arts, Niagara Falls, New York; Margy McClain, Urban Traditions, and Sarah R. Lea, both of Chicago, Illinois; Jane Viemeister, Albuquerque, New Mexico; Iowa City, Iowa, Public Library reference researchers, and others.

A Land of Turbulent History

In 1966 Poland celebrated a thousand years of nationhood. It marked that span from its conversion to Christianity under the great Prince Mieszko. The Polish people descended from Slavic tribes who lived in the forests along the Vistula River. One tribe was called the Polanie, meaning "people who live in the fields." Once nomadic, they built towns called *grody*, protected by wooden palisades. One of the most important, and the first capital of Poland, was *Gniezno* ("the nest").

Mieszko converted to Christianity when he married a Czech princess in 966. The marriage linked the destiny of Poland to the West. Their son, King Bolesław the Brave (reigned 992-1025), extended Polish power, but his descendants fought among themselves, dividing the country into small territories.

The Tatars, fierce fighters from the east, invaded Poland in 1241, laying waste to the city of Kraków, an event commemorated to this day, every hour on the hour, by a broken-off trumpet call from a tower in the great square of Kraków. The sudden break simulates the silencing of the trumpeter by a Tatar arrow.

Under Władysław I Łokietek, who ruled from 1320 to 1333, the nation was united again. His son, Kazimierz III Wielki (Casimir the Great), who ruled from 1333 to 1370, built well. According to a Polish proverb, he "found a wooden Poland and left her fortified in stone." There were no wars during his reign, and he made Poland strong economically. He also codified the laws for the first time, and founded the University of Kraków in 1364. Because he was childless, his nephew and successor, King Louis of Hungary, became an absentee monarch. Louis had no sons, and the Poles agreed to accept his daughter Jadwiga as his successor. Her marriage to Jagiełło of Lithuania in 1386 united Poland and Lithuania, beginning the Jagiellonian dynasty that lasted nearly two hundred years, a time of growth and prosperity. Successive wars with the Turks and the Russians caused Polish rulers to cede more rights to the nobles. The last of the Jagiełłos, Sigismund II Augustus (1548-1572), gave great economic power to the nobles. The

5

Italian Renaissance with its architecture was introduced into Poland in the sixteenth century. Protestantism made headway when the nobles coveted the power and property of the Church, but the Jesuits campaigned aggressively and Catholicism prevailed.

The Reformation, the Catholic Counter Reformation, and the war with Ivan the Terrible (1557-1582) of Russia followed. By defeating the Russians, Poland acquired Livonia and Latvia. The Lithuanian nobility joined Poland in 1569, the year of the beginning of the first Polish Republic and the creation of the Polish parliament, the *Sejm*. That body functioned remarkably well for decades, until stubbing its toe in 1652 by decreeing that a single vote could defeat any issue. This requirement of unanimity was too stringent for mortals, and the *Sejm* was frequently paralyzed. Even so, the first Polish Republic lasted until 1795.

In the years of the Republic, eleven Polish kings were elected. From 1669 to 1673, Michał Korybut Wiśniowiecki held the throne, losing Podolia to the Turks and the Ukraine to the Cossacks and Russia. John III Sobieski, ruling from 1674 to 1696, defeated the Turks at the Battle of Vienna in 1683. Without Poland, Christian Western Europe could not have repelled the Turkish invasion. This was the high point of Polish power. The seven decades after Sobieski's death brought declining national strength under non-Polish monarchs.

In the first of the three partitions of Poland, in 1773, Prussia took Polish Prussia except Gdańsk (Danzig) and Toruń. Austria took Red Ruthenia and western Podolia with Lwów and Kraków. Russia took White Ruthenia and all lands east of the Dvina and Dniepr rivers. In 1788, Prussia offered Poland an alliance, but later betrayed the Poles, and the second partition occurred January 23, 1793. Prussia took Gdańsk and Toruń as well as Great Poland, and Russia acquired most of Lithuania and western Ukraine. Poland became a puppet state. A national revolt in 1794, led by Tadeusz Kościuszko, a hero of the American Revolution, failed, and the third partition occurred October 24, 1795. With that, Poland was no longer on the map, and the last king of Poland, Stanisław Poniatowski, a former lover of Catherine the Great of Russia, abdicated.

Dreams of freedom refused to die, however. Poles took heart when Napoleon made Warsaw a grand duchy (1807-1815). The

1812 *Sejm* made itself into a General Confederation of Poland for reviving the Polish-Lithuanian Commonwealth. In 1815 Alexander I of Russia gave Russian Poland a constitution and a new name, the Kingdom of Poland within the Russian Empire. This designation would last until 1916. The passion for independence broke out in the November Insurrection of 1830, an uprising that failed and resulted in mass emigration. Those remaining in Russian Poland simmered under oppression until 1863, when a second revolution, the January Insurrection, was mounted. The immediate cause was forced conscription of Poles into the Russian army.

People in the Grand Duchy of Poznań and Polish provinces within the Kingdom of Prussia were deprived of many rights and freedoms between 1815 and 1918. Kraków was a free city, a joint protectorate of Austria, Prussia, and Russia, from 1815 until 1846, when Kraków armed forces failed in an offensive on Warsaw. Kraków was then annexed by Austria. Austria also controlled Galicia and Lodomeria or Little Poland *(Małopolska)* until 1918.

At the beginning of the twentieth century, the Russians were busy at home, and the Poles, holding strikes and demonstrations, won the right to organize trade unions, set up cultural associations, and open schools where students could be taught in Polish.

Led by Józef Piłsudski, Polish soldiers fought against Russian occupying forces during World War I. When the Russians were driven from Poland, the Germans moved in. In 1916, the Germans and Austrians wanted the Poles to swear loyalty to the German emperor and serve in the German army. Piłsudski and his followers refused to fight against the French and the English. He and many of his men were imprisoned.

In 1917, President Woodrow Wilson called for a united and independent Poland, and the Polish Republic was proclaimed on November 11, 1918. Piłsudski was chief of state. His choice for prime minister, Jędrzej Moraczewski, a colorless Socialist, was ineffective. Moraczewski was replaced in January 1919 by Ignacy Jan Paderewski, the famed pianist.

After defeating the White army, Lenin's Bolshevik army drove the Ukrainian troops of Ataman Semyon Petlura from Kiev. Piłsudski came to Petlura's aid, and his troops marched into Kiev in May 1920. Within three months Bolshevik troops, in retaliation,

7

advanced to the outskirts of Warsaw. The Bolsheviks proclaimed victory, but within a few days, Piłsudski and his Polish troops from the Ukraine arrived in Warsaw and defeated the Bolsheviks. An armistice was signed in October 1920.

As Poland worked to develop her economy, government, transportation, and education, war was on the way. Hitler invaded Czechoslovakia in 1938. Refusing to give up Gdańsk, Poland was invaded by the Nazis September 1, 1939, and the Soviets invaded September 17, 1939, deporting large numbers of Poles to Siberia.

In Poland, the Nazis built death and concentration camps at Auschwitz, Treblinka, Majdanek, and elsewhere, which became eternal symbols of infamy. The Jews of the Warsaw ghetto held out against the Nazis for a month in the spring of 1943. That same spring, Nazi soldiers discovered the mass graves of more than forty-two hundred Polish officers in the Soviet Union—in the Katyń forest near Smolensk. They had been murdered by the Russians in April 1940, each in full uniform, each shot in the head.

After the Nazis attacked Russia in 1941, the Soviets released many of their Polish prisoners to form a Polish army under General Władysław Anders. This army fought with the Allies in North Germany and Italy, including the hard-won victory over the Nazis at Monte Cassino. There were still enough Polish prisoners in the Soviet Union to form another army under General Berling, which fought alongside the Red Army all the way to Berlin.

Between 1939 and 1945 Poland lost 22 percent of its population. Among the estimated three million Poles who lost their lives were 40 percent of the nation's university professors. Nearly three million Jews were murdered, including those who had fled from Nazi Germany to Poland. Almost all of the gypsies were killed, and uncounted anti-Nazi Germans were shipped to Poland and exterminated. A quarter-million Polish children were deported to Germany to offset population losses there.

In August 1944, with the Red Army only twelve kilometers from Warsaw, the Poles staged an uprising to drive the Nazis out of the city. For two months, the Russians waited on the east bank of the Vistula River while the Nazis systematically demolished Warsaw.

During the war, the Polish government established itself in London, and from there it argued its boundary dispute with the

Soviets. The matter was settled in 1945 at Yalta in accordance with Soviet wishes, and the Third Polish Peoples' Republic was created. At Potsdam later that year, Poland's western border was fixed, restoring lost territory. In Lublin, Polish Communists formed the Polish Committee of National Liberation, which the Russians wanted to be the new government of Poland. The Allies insisted on broadening the committee, but Russian views prevailed.

After 1948, the Communists controlled Poland 's political and economic life. Many farmers were forced to give up their lands to state farms. Stefan Cardinal Wyszyński, head of the Catholic Church, was imprisoned. Private businesses were taken over by the state. By 1961 teaching religion in schools was forbidden.

The Poles restored and rebuilt Warsaw after World War II, but they had very little for themselves. In 1970 food prices increased dramatically, and workers who wanted better lives engaged in strikes and riots, particularly in Gdańsk. Władysław Gomułka resigned as head of the Polish Communist party. Lech Wałęsa, a shipyard electrician, was watching and learning.

Effectively led by Wałęsa, the 1980 strike at the Gdańsk shipyard indicated that a new day was dawning, but the triumphant Solidarity labor union was declared illegal in 1981 during a reign of martial law. Wałęsa was imprisoned many times, then released and rearrested. Martial law was lifted in 1983. A pro-Solidarity priest, Father Jerzy Popiełuszko, was murdered October 23, 1984, and was mourned internationally.

In 1989, the Polish government legalized Solidarity, which won many parliamentary seats in national elections. Wałęsa was elected president of Poland in 1990. Soviet troops withdrew from Poland in 1991, and the Warsaw Pact was dissolved.

Communist governments throughout Eastern Europe fell peacefully in the "velvet revolution." New governments, including that of Wałęsa, struggled to develop market economies. With inflation and unemployment rates high, Poles in 1993 gave parliamentary control to two parties dominated by former Communists and replaced Wałęsa as president in 1995 with a former Communist.

While some worried that the country might undergo a "velvet revolution" in reverse, the Polish people seemed firmly committed to freedom and democracy.

9

The White Eagle of Poland

A modern version of the White Eagle, in stained glass, is at the National Shrine of Our Lady of Częstochowa at Doylestown, Pennsylvania.

The white eagle on a crimson field that symbolizes the courage and freedom of Poland had its origins in the time of Lech, the legendary first Duke of Poland. As leader of the western Slavs, Lech united the tribes and maintained a strong army to defend his people against invasion. He became so famous that his name was attached to the land. The Turks called Poland *Lechistan* (the country of Lech), and the Russians called the Poles *Lachi*.

One fine spring day, the legend tells us, Lech and his court went hawking. Choosing to be alone, Lech rode toward a distant hill, where he spied an eagle's nest on a rocky crag. A noble white eagle sat there, surrounded by her young. Lech, who loved falconry and had trained many kinds of birds to hunt, yearned to train a young eagle. He coveted one of the white eaglets for that purpose.

Jumping from his horse, he climbed toward the nest. He tried to frighten the eagle away, but she would not leave the nest. When he stretched a hand to her, she pecked at him in warning. Lech pulled his dagger and held it on her while he reached for an eaglet with the other hand. She attacked him fiercely. The battle was on, and both were wounded. Seeing the bright blood on the eagle mother's white breast, Lech was touched by her courage and ashamed of trying to take what was so dear to her.

He climbed down, and as he walked away he gazed out over his beautiful country, a land he would defend as fiercely as the eagle defended her nest. As the eagle had shed her blood for her young, he would shed his own blood for Poland.

Thus Lech chose the white eagle as the badge of Poland, the token of freedom for which all Poles would shed their blood, and the blood on her white feathers would stand for bravery.

Loving the hill where he had found the nest, Lech ordered a castle to be built there, and then a city called *Gniezno* (the nest) grew on the site.

For at least a thousand years the White Eagle has flown on the banners of Poland, exhibiting the national colors of red and white. In past centuries the eagle wore on its head a crown as the emblem of the rulers, with each dynasty having a different emblem. For the 136 years that Poland was not on the maps of Europe, there was no eagle; it was banned by the occupying powers. With the re-emergence of Poland as a nation from 1918 to 1939, the eagle was royally crowned. During World War II, the Nazis banned the eagle. The Communists after the war allowed the eagle but took away her crown. When the Soviet Union and Warsaw Pact collapsed, the Poles recrowned their white eagle. It remains the proud symbol of high places and of Polish history and resolve.

The Polish eagle has its crown in this tribute to Paderewski placed by the Polish American Congress in the Shrine-church of Our Lady of Częstochowa in Doylestown, Pennsylvania.

11

Heroes in America

Tadeusz Kościuszko

Kazimierz Pułaski

Tadeusz Kościuszko

Tadeusz Kościuszko, a quiet hero of the American Revolutionary War, lacked the dash of Kazimierz Pułaski but earned Thomas Jefferson's praise as "the truest son of liberty I have ever known."

The son of an impoverished small landholder, he was born February 12, 1746, in Polish Lithuania. The turbulent microcosm of his native village, with Jews, Ruthenians, Lithuanians, Uniats, Roman Catholics, Greek Orthodox, Tatars, Cossacks, and Armenians, was ideal preparation for the American melting pot.

Kościuszko attended the Jesuit College at Brześć, graduated from Warsaw's Royal College in 1769, and then studied in England, Germany, and France on a military scholarship. He returned to Poland in 1774 and became a captain of artillery. Two years later, he volunteered to serve in the American Revolutionary Army.

He arrived in Philadelphia in the summer of 1776 far more qualified than any staff officer George Washington possessed. His first job was to build sea forts on Billingsport Island, to keep British ships out of the Delaware River. Next, he obstructed the advance of General Burgoyne at Ticonderoga and made the American position impregnable, ensuring their first great victory of the war.

His true monument in America is West Point, which he fortified so well between 1778 and 1780 that it was called the "American Gibraltar." He also designed a huge chain to bar the Hudson River, each link weighing 140 pounds.

For the war in the South, Kościuszko designed flatboats on quickly detachable wheels and axles to move on land or water. This helped the Americans escape the British General Charles Cornwallis, who surrendered at Yorktown in October 1781.

During the remainder of the war, Kościuszko fought more as a soldier than as a military engineer. He declined promotions and served without pay. At Fraunces Tavern in New York on December 4, 1783, Washington gave his farewell to his officers and presented his own sword, engraved to commemorate the occasion, to Kościuszko. Lafayette and Steuben, the French and German generals, were the only other foreigners present. Congress passed a resolution stating its "high sense" of Kościusko's "long and meritorious service," and he was awarded citizenship in the new nation.

Kościuszko sailed home in 1784 to join the Polish revolutionary movement. He helped lead the army against Russian invaders in 1792, becoming a national leader after the Second Partition of 1793.

On the battlefield he wore his American uniform and carried George Washington's sword, but in 1794 his army was beaten by the Russians and Prussians. He was slashed in the face by a Cossack saber, shot in the thigh by a cannon ball, and bayoneted three times where he lay.

Surviving, he spent two years in a Russian prison. The death of Catherine II of Russia led to his release, and in 1797, he returned to America and a hero's welcome. Congress gave him his long-overdue military pay plus interest, and he planned to buy a farm near Saratoga Springs, New York. This was not to be.

Thomas Jefferson asked his help in persuading Napoleon to

stop harassing American shipping, and Kościuszko departed for Europe secretly to carry out this mission. Before he left he drew a will directing that all his American assets be used to free and educate black slaves, this system being his only complaint against a land he loved nearly as much as his own lost Poland.

Kościuszko retired in Switzerland, writing (among other works) his *Manoeuvres of Horse Artillery*, which was used by the United States War Department until the Civil War.

Kościuszko died October 15, 1817, in Soleure, or Solothurn, Switzerland. His heart is buried in Switzerland, and his body lies in the royal crypt of the Wawel Castle in Kraków. The people of Poland carried soil from every Polish battlefield where he fought to raise a mountain of honor to this great patriot on the banks of the Vistula in Kraków.

An Australian mountain bears his name with its spelling intact, but an Indiana county and a Mississippi town have spelled it Kociusko. Self-effacing as he was, Tadeusz Kościuszko probably wouldn't have minded.

Kazimierz Pułaski

Seven American counties, five towns, a highway, and countless streets are named for Brigadier General Count Kazimierz Pułaski of Poland, who served brilliantly under Washington in the American Revolution.

Pułaski, whose first name was Anglicized to Casimir in this country, was born in 1747 at Winiary, about forty miles from Warsaw. He was the hero of the 1768 Polish insurrection, defending Berdyczew in 1768 and Częstochowa in 1770-1771 against Russian attacks. Failure of his attempt to kidnap King Stanisław August Poniatowski in 1771 forced him into exile.

He fled to Turkey in 1772, the time of the first partition of Poland, and spent two years trying to incite the Turks to attack Russia, Poland's conqueror. Fighting Russians was nothing new to Pułaski; a rumor that the British would hire Russian mercenaries to put down the American rebellion soon proved an inducement for him to go to America.

Pułaski met Benjamin Franklin in Paris in 1776. Bearing a letter from Franklin, he arrived at Boston in July 1777 and met George

14

Washington at Neshaminy Falls in Pennsylvania.

Franklin wrote to Washington: "Count Pułaski, an officer famous throughout Europe for his bravery and conduct in the defense of the liberties of his country against three invading powers . . . may be highly useful to our service." Indeed he was.

Pułaski, a cavalry and guerrilla warfare expert, asked for thirty men to sweep the British line, and extricated the Americans from a British trap in the Battle of Brandywine. He was promoted from chief of dragoons to brigadier general and chief of cavalry. He fought at Germantown (a Philadelphia suburb) in 1777-1778.

American soldiers disliked taking orders from a foreigner, so Pułaski, with permission, formed his own corps, the Pułaski Legion. The recruits included Polish, French, and German officers and German-American lancers and riflemen. Among them was "Light Horse" Harry Lee, father of Robert E. Lee, the great American general who headed the Confederate armies in the Civil War.

Pułaski taught his men to ride Cossack style, and the Moravian Sisters of Bethlehem, Pennsylvania, sewed them a brilliant banner. The Pułaski Legion saw action in the defense of Charleston in 1779. In battle at Savannah, an American deserter had betrayed army plans to the British, and Pułaski sought to rally the American troops by leading the charge against the British. He wore a splendid hussar's uniform with a plume and saber, which made him easy to see and follow despite the smoke of battle. After he had restored order, he was shot in the thigh and fell from his horse. Men from his legion carried him from the field. He was taken to the American ship *Wasp,* and died aboard on October 11, 1779, as it neared Charleston, where he would have received medical care.

Pułaski's larger-than-life presence in the world made his death dramatic and inspiring to the comrades he left behind. He had explained to George Washington why he was willing to join a seemingly lost cause: "Wherever men can fight for liberty, that is also our fight and our place."

Congress appointed a committee to plan a monument to Pułaski, the first of many to be raised to him by Americans. His service in the American Revolution is an important part of the freedom Americans enjoy today.

Decades of Immigration

In America you can reach your dreams. This is not a privilege for a select few, but a goal reachable by all. The United States gives people a chance to fulfill their needs in education, travel, culture, and all the things that are so much more important than material goods.

—Andrzej Nowak
Guide, Polish Museum of America
1986 immigrant from Poland

A Polish publisher in Spain had spread the news of Columbus's discovery of America, and in 1532 Nicholas Copernicus, the great Polish astronomer, wrote a book chapter on America. Because Poland was at that time enjoying its rich Renaissance, the allure of the New World was less than strong, but far from nonexistent.

Captain John Smith of Jamestown, the earliest permanent settlement in America, had fought with the Poles against the Turks in Hungary, and he knew of Polish skills in glass-blowing. He persuaded the London Company to hire some Poles to bring that industry to Jamestown. In 1609, when some Indians planned to ambush Captain Smith, it was Poles who helped save his life and captured the Indians' chief.

In 1619, the Poles, working in pitch, tar and soap-ash manufacture, threatened to strike if they were not allowed to vote for their representatives to the Virginia House of Burgesses. This was the first labor protest by Poles in America, and the Poles were given the right to vote.

Dr. Aleksander Karol Kurcjusz (Curtius), a Polish physician and surgeon, settled in New Amsterdam (later New York) and founded the first classical Latin school there.

Daniel Litscho, as an aide to Governor Peter Stuyvesant of New Amsterdam, helped in the 1655 conquest of New Sweden, an area north of the present Wilmington, Delaware. Poles mentioned in the annals of the Colony of New Sweden include a Polish Lutheran minister. A Polish officer close to Stuyvesant was Captain Marcin Krygier, commander of Fort Casimir, named for a famed Polish king and the first Polish place name in the New World.

Olbracht Zaborowski (Zabriskie), who arrived in America in 1662, had such a strong affinity for the Algonquin Indians that he allowed his son to live with them for seven years to learn their ways. The boy grew up to be the Dutch colony's negotiator with the Indians. Antoni Sądowski (Sandusky) bought land along the Schuylkill River in Pennsylvania in 1712 and pressed on to a Daniel Boone style of life in the wilderness. Rev. Christian Frederick Post, born in Poland in 1710, became a missionary to the Polish Moravian Church in America and to the Indians.

While never setting foot in America, Pieter Stadnitski of Amsterdam, Holland, who was of Polish descent, found a source of credit for the Americans and was an organizer of the Holland Land Company for speculations in "the wild lands in the United States." In Buffalo, New York, a street and a senior citizens' complex are named for him.

After the pope disbanded the Society of Jesus in Poland in the late eighteenth century, Jesuit priests came to Philadelphia. Among them was Rev. Francis Dzierożyński, credited with saving the American Jesuit movement from extinction.

A few Polish immigrants came to America in the Napoleonic era. Poles sent to Santo Domingo to put down a slave revolt in 1802 did so unwillingly, and 240 of them were then permitted to come to the United States. In 1817, Congress granted ninety-two thousand acres in Alabama to French and Polish exiles of the Napoleonic wars.

In 1830, upon learning that the Russian command was sending them to Paris to put down a revolt, Polish cadets rebelled in the "November Uprising." Prominent Americans enlisted aid for their cause, and 234 defeated rebels arrived in New York in 1834.

In 1842 the Association of Poles in America was founded, and a decade later the Democratic Society of Polish Exiles was formed to denounce slavery. The first Polish language newspapers were started in this era, and Polish immigrants advertised their services as teachers of dancing, riding, fencing, and languages.

Anthony Schermann (Smarzewski) of Chicago reportedly

brought 100,000 Poles to America. A carpenter and businessman, he had been active in the 1830 Polish insurrection.

Henryk Dmochowski (Sanders), a Polish-American sculptor, included Tadeusz Kościuszko and Casimir Pułaski among Revolutionary heroes of whom he sculpted busts for the rotunda of the nation's Capitol.

Dr. Feliks Paul Wierzbicki, a Polish-American physician, fought in the Mexican War and then went to California, where he wrote his *Guide to the Gold Region*, the first book printed west of the Rocky Mountains.

A Polish soldier, Lieutenant Feliks Andrzej Wardzinski, is credited with capturing Santa Anna, president of Mexico, at San Jacinto, and bringing him to General Sam Houston, in the battle that won Texas its independence from Mexico.

Among remarkable Polish women who came to America was Ernestine Louise S. Potowska-Rose, who arrived in 1836, became a campaigner for women's rights and was an Abolitionist (one of the anti-slavery movements). In 1853 Dr. Maria Zakrzewska immigrated and six years later founded the Boston hospital that became the New England Hospital for Women and Children. She, too, was an Abolitionist.

A Pole, Henry Kalussowski, translated Russian to English during the 1867 negotiations that followed Russia's offer to sell Alaska to the United States. Poles had arrived in both Alaska and California in the ninety years or so of Russian colonization. They kept coming after the American purchase. There once was a town called Pollasky in California's Fresno County, founded in 1846 by Mark Pulaski. Many Poles came to California during the 1849 gold rush.

In 1854, about eight hundred Poles—one hundred families— from Upper Silesia arrived at the port of Galveston, Texas. Led by Father Leopold Moczygemba, a Conventual Franciscan, they hired Mexican carts to haul their farm implements, featherbeds, and, from their parish church in Poland, a heavy cross and a bell. Then they walked—some in boots, some barefoot—two hundred miles to the sites of their settlement. During this walk there were births and deaths, hunger and exposure. They arrived on Christmas Eve, 1854. Beneath a large oak they offered their first Midnight Mass, placing their new community under the patronage of the Immaculate Conception. Thus was founded the town of Panna Maria (Virgin Mary), Texas, the oldest Polish settlement in America. The families camped out until they could put up huts of mud, straw or wood, later building in stone. These Polish immigrants fled from Prussian oppression and came to Texas to gain economic, political, and religious freedom. Here they could even fly the flag of Poland, which was forbidden in their homeland. Despite hardships, they built a stable community, aided in settling other frontiers, pioneered in education, and gave Texas many patriotic, dedicated citizens. They built a church in 1856, and St. Joseph's School in 1858. It was the first Polish school in America. Today the building houses the Museum of the Panna Maria Historical Association.

In 1966, the millennium of Poland's Christianity, President Lyndon B. Johnson accepted from American Polonia a mosaic of Our Lady of Czestochowa, and asked that it be placed in the Church at Panna Maria. Other Polish settlements in Texas were started in San Antonio, Yorktown, Bandera, Saint Hedwig, Częstochowa, Kościuszko, Falls City, Polonia, and Pawelekville.

By the time of the Civil War, about thirty thousand Poles had arrived in the United States. About five thousand fought in the Union Army, and one thousand in the Confederate forces. The Union Army had 166 Polish-American officers and the Confederacy had 40. Polish Americans, including nuns, were among the women who served by caring for the wounded on the battlefields. The oldest Polish soldier was Joseph Krokowski, sixty-one, of Jones County, Iowa. The youngest were three sixteen-year-olds— Edmund L. G. Zalenski, Louis A. Senteller, and Stanislaus Rydzewski, all of New York state. The last surviving Polish-American veteran of the Civil War was August Romanowski, who died in 1929 at age 101, at Chippewa Falls, Wisconsin.

Brigadier General Włodzimierz Krzyżanowski distinguished himself for the Union and became the first governor of the Alaska territory. Jozef Karge was an expert cavalryman who became a professor of languages at Princeton.

Kacper Tochman, once an officer in the Polish army, fought for the Confederacy. Leon Jastremski, who enlisted in Tochman's "Polish brigade," rose from private to brigadier general in the Louisiana National Guard, became mayor of Baton Rouge in 1876, and seemed to be winning his campaign for the governorship of Louisiana when he died in 1907.

The true flood of immigration began in the 1880s, when one shipload of Poles after another arrived in American harbors. In many cases a young man came first, saved his money, and hired a professional scribe to ask a girl from his village in Poland to come to America and be his wife. By the turn of the century, two and a half million Poles had immigrated to the United States.

Most arrived too late for the best homesteading opportunities. They established communities near the mines, the quarries, and the steel furnaces, bringing to their new jobs incredible strength and enthusiasm for work. Poland, split up by its oppressors, had offered them nothing. German law took the peasants' land away. Russian serfdom still was strong in the memories of immigrants. Austrian Galicia was impoverished. The anthracite fields of Pennsylvania employed many, as did the textile mills of New England, the lumber and railroad industries of the American West, the steel mills of the Midwest and East, slaughterhouses in Chicago and elsewhere, and loading docks in New Jersey. Everyone in the family worked. Many immigrant women ran boarding houses.

From the beginning, social life for Polonia revolved around the parish church and school. The Polish Americans constructed beautiful churches, some of them large. St. Stanislaus Church in Buffalo, New York, at one time served a parish of thirty-five thousand Polish Americans with a dual upper and lower church. Insurance fraternals provided security and additional social life.

In America, Poles found the Catholic churches dominated by the Irish, who had arrived first. The differences possibly could have been resolved, but were not. The Irish accused the Polish Catholics of "foreignizing" and the Poles believed that all Catholics should be able to worship in their own languages. Eventually, in 1904, a major group of Catholics formed the Polish National Catholic Church, the first schism in the Roman Catholic Church in decades. Today the Polish National Catholic Church has some 300,000 members with its own hierarchy and with headquarters in Scranton, Pennsylvania. Rome took a new look at Polish-American Catholicism, naming a few more Polish priests who became bishops. Rev. Paul Rhode of Chicago became the first Polish bishop in 1908. Not until 1967, however—long after the break—was a Polish American elevated to cardinal—John Cardinal Krol of Philadelphia, now emeritus. One of every five Roman Catholics in the United States is of Polish descent.

During labor disputes, Polish workers could always be found in the thick of the battle. The New Year's Day 1888 strike of coal miners of the Shenandoah Valley was fatal to a dozen Polish Americans. In 1894 a tenth of Coxey's Army of the unemployed was Polish. Their zeal produced men like David Dubinsky, the fiery labor leader of the 1930s.

John Smulski of Chicago organized a Polish National Committee for Polish independence and helped recruit 26,000 Polish Americans for the Blue Army, which fought in France under General Józef Haller during World War I.

Ignacy Paderewski, the pianist and Polish statesman, lobbied Washington and the American public on behalf of Poland. After World War I, President Woodrow Wilson succeeded in winning independence for Poland and Czechoslovakia. Impressive monuments to President Wilson in both countries were among the first things destroyed by the Nazis in World War II.

The Nazi invasion of Poland in September 1939 aroused deep feelings among Polish Americans. The October Pulaski Day parade along New York's Fifth Avenue that year involved 200,000 marchers. An estimated twelve percent of United States armed forces in World War II were Polish Americans. They served with distinction, contributing a number of high-ranking officers and the leading American air ace, Francis S. Gabreski, who won twelve Distinguished Flying Crosses.

During and after World War II, members of the Polish intelligentsia arrived in the United States as refugees. They included: Dr. Ludwik Gross and Dr. Hilary Koprowski, medical scientists doing research in cancer and virology; Dr. Walter Golaski, who developed a vascular prosthesis used in heart surgery; Zbysław M. Roehr, who invented the disposable hypodermic needle and syringe; Antoni Zygmund, mathematician; Dr. Tadeusz Sendzimir, an inventor who contributed greatly to the steel industry; Aleksander de Seversky, who founded the Republic Aircraft Corporation; Mieczysław Bekker, who invented the Moon Rover used on the

1971 Apollo flight; and Wanda Landowska, one of the greatest harpsichordists the world has known.

In 1948 the Displaced Persons Act opened immigration to Europe's homeless, and a new wave of Polish arrivals began with the docking of the *General Black*, an old troopship. The passengers called themselves the "black generals."

Since the 1960s a steady flow of Polish creative artists has been enriching American culture—jazz musicians, conductors, artists, writers, actors, and directors.

The early Polish immigrants were cut from different cloth than were the later immigrants. Because of their homeland's turbulent history, they have not remembered the same Poland, but they have shared a strong bond in following the Roman Catholic faith, with a rich folk art tradition in their liturgy and daily life.

The government's crushing of the Solidarity union movement created one million more Polish immigrants for America, Australia, Canada, and other countries. The Polish Communist regime gave many Solidarity workers the option of a long prison sentence or a passport to emigrate. As a result, there are an estimated 100,000 new Polish immigrants in Chicago, the city with forty blocks of Polish-American businesses. Another estimated 100,000 live near Greenpoint, a part of Brooklyn, New York.

States with large populations of Polish Americans include Michigan, Ohio, Illinois, Indiana, Wisconsin, Pennsylvania, New York, and New Jersey. The Polish Room of the University of Pittsburgh depicts a Golden Age of Poland, the sixteenth century. Its decorations were inspired by Wawel Castle in Kraków.

In 1925 in New York City Stephen Mizwa founded the prestigious Kościuszko Foundation, which supports educational and cultural activities. Mizwa came to the United States in 1910, graduated from Amherst College, and earned a master's degree from Harvard College. The foundation sponsors exchanges of professors and scholars between Poland and the United States.

Europe has known the Poles as a proud people who retained identity under the most repressive conditions. Their energy, curiosity, and independence are well-suited to America, and they have made their mark in every area of life.

How can Polish Americans be successful, influential, and modern in American society while maintaining their identity as Polish Americans? The Reverend Leonard F. Chrobot, professor of sociology at Saint Mary's College, Orchard Lake, Michigan, says the answer is education.

Our Challenge

by Reverend Leonard F. Chrobot

We live in a free society with all kinds of opportunities for education. Polish Americans should take advantage of these opportunities. If our children have intellectual ability, we should help them develop it to its ultimate potential.

We as Polish Americans desperately need verbal skills, the ability to put into words what it is that we feel down deep in our hearts—our values—so other people can understand what we believe. I believe America is searching for these kinds of values today.

I believe I have a serious obligation before God, because of my parents and grandparents, to contribute to this emerging American culture. I have an obligation to the gnarled hands and stooped backs of my grandparents, who worked long and difficult hours on farm and in factory so that their children and grandchildren would have a better world. I thank God for them every day. I owe them something. They paid a great price for me to be here today. My only tribute to them would be to contribute to the growth and development of our Polish cultural heritage in America today. America is my country. I am not a Pole living in America, I am an American, but not just any kind of an American.

I am an American of Polish descent, of Polish cultural heritage. I want to cherish that heritage, and I want to teach it to other people so that they can cherish it the same way that I do. This is our task. This is our opportunity. This is our challenge.

My Mother Came from Poland

By Alice Wadowski-Bak

My mother, Katherine Theresa Wadowski (Katarzyna Grabiec Wadowska) was born August 6, 1898, in a village named after a hill, Gora (Hill) Ropczycka in Poland. The village is on several train stops on the line from Kraków. My mother, who left the village as a fifteen-year-old girl, drew a map of her village when I visited Poland. I figured after forty years and two wars there would be changes, but the stations were exactly as she remembered.

Kasia or Katie, as she was lovingly called, packed her straw basket suitcase, gathered her feather coverlet and said good-bye to her aunt and friends. A statue of the Blessed Mother was safely nestled inside the knot-tied coverlet. Her farewell gift, a lovely, floral shawl, was draped over her shoulders. Sometimes, she wrapped in its warmth by placing it on her head, allowing the fringe to gently fall on her arms and the shawl to cover her dark brown tresses and the hidden pocket that held the ticket for a seven-day sea voyage. Later, when she felt pangs of loneliness, the colors of the shawl would cheer her, and the flowers in the design would remind her of sun-filled days brimming with real blossoms.

The name rang like a bell tolling in her head—"Ameryka!" The awesome word made her tremble inside. The bigness of that land might swallow her. Kasia was traveling all alone, across Europe, across the ocean to another continent. Her only travels before were to the next village and to another town by foot, on a pilgrimage. She had never seen an ocean ship. She boarded the train that would take her to Germany and to the ship, the *Kaiser Wilhelm*, for its last voyage to America before the outbreak of the First World War.

Kasia's Story

Anxiety, fear, uncertainty. Will there be someone to meet me? How will I understand what they are saying? Where are the familiar voices, faces, and the language of my homeland? I feel so lost. I want to go home, but no one is there. My parents are dead. My stepbrother, who sent me passage, and his wife live in Indiana.

24

My sister, her husband and children live in Massachusetts. Only an aunt is in Poland, and there isn't work enough for my future. Many friends have left with their families before me, but they went to other cities, and I will be far from them. I have to keep going. Everyone has told me that it is a better life, with work, in Ameryka.

I feel excited with butterflies going wild in my stomach. I feel goose bumps for the wonder of actually going across the ocean. Me, going to Ameryka! I feel very much alone when I taste food I have never tasted before, when I see people dressed different from me and speaking languages I have never heard before. Will I be lost? How would anyone find me? Will I find work? Could I really understand how to do the work and do a good job at it?

I wish I could talk over these fears. Oh, if someone could speak my language to me now. What if someone steals my money? Who could I trust? Who could I tell and how could I tell them, when I can't even speak the language? My little Polish prayer book is a great comfort to me now. I have almost worn out the pages.

The train comes to a screeching halt and everyone hurries to the crowded custom lines. The waiting ship looms like a giant bird over the landscape, breathtaking and majestic. It will take me sailing over the seas to my new homeland! I heard that a storm at sea can toss everyone about without mercy. I hope I don't get seasick. I will pray that the ship doesn't sink—I can't swim!

I have a ship card and a tag with my destination pinned to my dress. I am careful not to let anything happen to it, or I might be sent to the wrong place and how could I ever let my brother know where I had gone? Maybe they would send me back to Poland. I would be so ashamed. People would think I was rejected or thrown out of Ameryka as an "undesirable." Everyone in the village would laugh at me. I could never go back.

In steerage, the lowest level on the ship, it is dark and the air is thick. As the ship moves out to sea, I get sick.

As night falls, I feel so lonely. Families huddle together and find safety in their numbers. I yearn to speak to someone, yet I am afraid. I draw the feather coverlet near on my lap and rest my head on it. I try to get some sleep but am afraid to close my eyes. When I do, the tears flow. I am so homesick now.

I can't eat. My stomach turns too much. They give me a banana with my lunch, but I never ate one before, so I give it away to make friends with a little girl and her family. I wonder what country they are from and if I will ever see them in Ameryka. All we can do is smile and talk a little with our fingers, but I know somebody a little now. I feel warm and safe.

We are urged to go up on deck for fresh air, but we cannot speak German to tell the crew that we are afraid of losing our places and possessions. All that we own is what we carry with us now.

***

On another ship, a young man of seventeen leaves the farmlands of Kelice, Poland, for the magical city of Niagara Falls, New York, in Ameryka. Michael Joseph Wadowski, leaving his sisters and mother behind, feels many of the emotions that Kasia feels. Although Michael is traveling with a fellow villager, both young men share uncertainty, excitement and fears. Europe is being tugged by the winds of an oncoming war. They worry about leaving families and friends behind in a troubled world.

—From a family history

Folk artist Alice Wadowski-Bak of Niagara Falls, New York

Caught in the Middle

When Nazi Germany invaded Poland September 1, 1939, and the Russians invaded sixteen days later, Poland became a battlefield and its people pawns in a war more horrible than the world had ever before known. William Nowysz, two years old when the war began, felt its effects first-hand by the age of four.

Russian soldiers were the first to arrive in the small village where Nowysz lived with his father, a Russian Orthodox priest, and his mother. The anti-cleric Russians soon took Nowysz's father into the garden and killed him.

Nowysz and his mother found refuge in the home of friends in the nearby village of Kobrin as the war raged around them.

"We were caught between the Russians and the Germans," said Nowysz, an architect now living in Iowa City, Iowa, and Boston, Massachusetts. Troops from both sides moved back and forth constantly until the German army suddenly overran the area.

All Poles were expected to house the invading Germans, and the household, which included two families of three each, gave up one of its five rooms to house about a half dozen German soldiers.

To Nowysz, "it was scary. They had helmets and rifles."

To young boys, however, rifles and bayonets also were "absolutely neat," so he and his friends one day sneaked into the Germans' room, sat down on the floor and played with a rifle. One of the boys pulled the trigger, shooting a hole in the ceiling. Nowysz's mother, Nina, and stepfather, Marion, were angry and terrified; the Germans had to account for every bullet.

"She (Nina) had to do a lot of talking," Nowysz said. "All the kids were in deep, deep trouble."

In the village, the Germans were increasingly anxious to find out who was Jewish. Occasionally, people were gathered up and sent away. The Russians had taken Polish people to Siberia. The Germans took them to work camps and factories. The villagers did not know about death camps, but Nowysz now believes a lot of the family's friends ended up there.

As the war gathered intensity, several families, including the

Nowyszes, decided to leave the village. They left in a caravan amid fighting and bombs, heading south and west to escape the war zone and stay away from the Russians. They traveled by train and picked up work wherever they could find it. The Germans detained anyone who had no permanent residence, so the families were caught up several times in work camps. Nowysz recalls jobs with a farmer in northern Germany and at a parachute factory. He remembers bombs falling on a barracks that housed the family.

Once, after being caught in Austria, the family was sorted and directed to trains at a station. The elder Nowyszes were concerned; they had heard rumors about people being sorted and put on trains. They located young William, who had already been sorted, and Marion ordered his wife and stepson to pick up their suitcases and run across the tracks. The Nowyszes escaped to a village, where villagers provided temporary shelter. The trains were headed for concentration camps.

As the family traveled about, Nowysz attended rigorous German schools. The system depended upon humiliation of students who didn't measure up, so Nowysz learned the German language in a hurry. He was fluent in German by the time the war ended.

At war's end, the family was in Bavaria, in the Alps, living in a room above the Swiss cheese factory where Marion worked until the war halted production. Soon trucks carrying United States soldiers arrived. "The kids thought (the arrival of the Allies) was terrific," said Nowysz, then eight years old. "The Germans had abandoned all their cars and other vehicles, and we thought they were neat to play with."

The family was shuttled to a displaced persons' camp in Germany and later to a camp run by the United Nations Relief Agency. Those in the camps were offered a choice: return to their homelands or emigrate. The Nowyszes opted for emigration—to Venezuela. The United States was second choice.

Nowysz doesn't know why his parents picked Venezuela, nor why they failed to get there. The Nowyszes headed for the United States in 1950, when a farmer from Idaho agreed to sponsor them.

A troop carrier, the General Sturgis, took them across the ocean, men and women on separate decks. Few passengers were prepared for the cold, so sailors on the ship supplied warm clothing.

Nowysz was issued a Navy pea jacket, which he still has.

For Nowysz, New York City was another new experience. He was surprised by the city's size, the numerous cars, the paved streets, the whiteness of the bread, and the multistory apartments. "I'd never lived in a place up in the air that much," he said.

The Nowyszes spent three days in the city waiting for their sponsor. When he didn't appear, Marion Nowysz called Polish friends in Muscatine, Iowa, who had emigrated two years earlier. The friends sent money for bus tickets to Muscatine.

In Muscatine, young Nowysz, who knew no English, attended a church school where a teacher spoke German. He graduated from the public high school, studied architecture at the University

Nina and Nickolai Scobie are shown with their infant son, Wasilli, in this portrait taken in about 1938 in Poland. Wasilli took his stepfather's last name, Nowysz, during the war and adopted William as a first name after his family came to the United States in 1950.

of Michigan and now practices in Iowa City. His buildings have won numerous architectural awards.

In 1978, after the death of his mother, Nowysz found a letter from an uncle in Scotland dated in 1972. Nowysz's late wife, Margaret, called information to get the uncle's telephone number in Glasgow and immediately had him on the telephone. The Nowyszes were soon exchanging visits with relatives Nowysz had not seen since he was a toddler.

Nowysz has more distant relatives in Poland, but he has not met them. His only visit to his homeland was during Communist rule, when free travel was not permitted.

Leadership from Polonia

Polonia: A term used to describe any group of people of Polish descent living elsewhere than in Poland.

Senator Barbara Mikulski

"My great-grandmother came to America from Poland at age sixteen with no money or job, looking for opportunity," says United States Senator Barbara Ann Mikulski.

Elected in 1986, Mikulski is the first woman to win a statewide election in Maryland, the first Democratic woman to win a Senate seat not previously held by her husband, and the first Democratic woman to serve in both houses of Congress.

In her high school years she worked in her parents' neighborhood grocery store in East Baltimore. A college graduate, she began her involvement in public affairs by leading opposition to a highway that would have destroyed the first home-ownership neighborhood for blacks in Baltimore. At one rally she said: "We didn't let the British take Fells point; we didn't let termites take Fells Point; and we're not going to let the State Roads Commission take Fells Point." Her side won, and Mikulski decided to run for Baltimore City Council. She knocked on 15,000 front doors and was elected.

Gen. John M. Shalikashvili, named head of NATO forces in 1992, was appointed chairman of the Joint Chiefs of Staff in 1993 by President Bill Clinton. Shalikashvili was born in Poland; his mother was Polish, and his father was a Georgian military officer. The family fled Poland in 1944, ahead of the approaching Russians.

Edmund S. Muskie was the first Polish American to become governor of a state (Maine). He also served as a United States senator and Secretary of State, and was the Democratic candidate for vice-president in 1968. His career surpassed the expectations of his father, Stefan Marciszewski, a tailor who came to the United States in 1903.

The first Polish American to hold a cabinet post was Dr. John Gronouski, who served as Postmaster General and United States ambassador to Poland. Gronouski also was dean of the Lyndon Johnson School for Public Affairs, and directed United States Information Agency broadcast services to Iron Curtain countries.

Dr. Zbigniew Brzezinski, President Jimmy Carter's National Security Council chairman, became the second Polish American to attain cabinet-level rank. Born in Poland, educated in Canada, where his father was in the Polish diplomatic corps, Brzezinski taught government at Harvard and Columbia University before joining Georgetown University's Center for Strategic International Studies. He was foreign policy adviser to three presidents.

Dan Rostenkowski, former Democratic congressman from Illinois, served as chairman of the House Ways and Means Committee. Another Polish American, Klement Zabłocki, has served as chairman of the House Foreign Relations Committee. In 1975, Mary Ann Krupsak became the first woman lieutenant governor of New York. It was the highest public office to which a Polish-American woman had ever been elected.

Mitchell Kobelinski of Chicago was appointed head of the Small Business Administration by President Gerald Ford.

Senator Barry Goldwater of Arizona was the 1964 Republican candidate for president, two generations after the immigration of his merchant grandfather, Michael Goldwasser.

America's Polonia has supplied many leaders in business and industry. Casimir S. Gzowski crossed into Canada before the Civil War, developed a railroad system and built an International Bridge over the Niagara River. He was knighted by Queen Victoria. Ralph Modjeski, son of the great Polish actress, built the Philadelphia-Camden bridge over the Delaware River. It opened in 1926 as the longest single-span suspension bridge in the world. Edward Piszek founded Mrs. Paul's Pies of Philadelphia and built it into a major company. Taking to the air like a true Polish eagle was Frank N. Piasecki, founder of the Piasecki Aircraft Corporation.

Orchard Lake Schools

Rev. Stanley E. Milewski, third from left, chancellor of Orchard Lake Schools, with priests and seminarians from Poland who would serve American parishes. Orchard Lake Schools includes a four-year prep school for young men, a coeducational four-year liberal arts college, and a seminary. Pictured above with Father Milewski are, from left: Mirosław Stelmaszczyk, Rev. Ryszard Goluch, Andrzej Malarz, Tadeusz Świerz, and Rev. Stanisław Drewniak.

Pope John Paul II has called SS. Cyril & Methodius Seminary, Orchard Lake, Michigan, "the most beautiful Polish seminary in the whole world." The setting is a gem, with sparkling waters, green vistas, peaceful bells, and the glowing copper embrace of Our Lady of Orchard Lake on the facade of her contemporary shrine chapel, built in 1963.

Thousands of priests and lay leaders have studied at Orchard Lake, where the seminary is now related to Saint Mary's College, a four-year coeducational Catholic liberal arts college, and Saint Mary's Preparatory, a highly accredited four-year prep school for young men.

Besides propagating the faith in Polish terms, the purpose of the Orchard Lake Schools is to enrich American culture with the best of the Polish heritage. This effort is enhanced by the Center for Polish Studies and Culture, the Polish American Liturgical Center, and the Pope John Paul II Center.

The seminary was born of the need for priests to care for Polish immigrants, whose spiritual needs were soon served by nine hundred churches. In January 1879 Father Leopold Moczygemba, the Polish priest who had led his flock to Texas in 1854, obtained permission from Pope Leo XIII to establish a seminary in the United States. In 1884 Father Moczygemba entrusted the papal charter to Father Joseph Dąbrowski.

Father Dąbrowski was born in Zółtance in 1842, was schooled in Lublin, and seemed headed for a career as an engineer. His participation in the failed January Insurrection of 1863 forced him to leave Poland. He went to Dresden, Switzerland, and finally to Rome, where he prepared for the priesthood. He arrived in the United States in 1869.

Nebraska land had been bought for a seminary, but the pattern of Polish immigration did not justify that site nor one in rural Wisconsin. Father Dąbrowski founded the Motherhouse of the Felician Sisters in Detroit, making his home there and seeking to start a theological seminary in that city of many Poles. He bought land on St. Aubin Avenue, and ground was broken May 19, 1885, for a seminary building. The cornerstone was laid that July, and the seminary was dedicated to SS. Cyril and Methodius, Apostles to the Slavs. It was more commonly referred to as "the Polish Seminary." Classes began in December 1886. The seminary attracted other nationalities; at the 1894 commencement, students spoke in nine languages.

In 1896, night classes for immigrants began. Despite added wings and a new classroom-gymnasium the school was overcrowded. That problem was solved by the 1909 purchase of the Michigan Military Academy in Orchard Lake. The site boasted eight Gothic and Romanesque revival buildings, including "the

Castle"—chapel, canteen, and faculty living quarters. A 70-acre farm was part of the property, and in the early years it supplied much of the institution's food.

Father Witold Buhaczkowski succeeded Father Dąbrowski as rector, and Minnesota-born Father Michael Grupa served from 1917 to 1932. Then came Father Anthony Kłowo, a Polish-born graduate of Orchard Lake Seminary, who was rector from 1932-1937. The fifth rector (1937-1943) was Pennsylvania-born Ladislaus Krzyżosiak, also an Orchard Lake graduate.

Father Edward Szumal served from 1943 to 1955, and Father Wallace Filipowicz led the schools until his death in 1967. Father Walter Ziemba became rector-president-superintendent until his resignation in 1977, when Father Stanley E. Milewski was elected the first chancellor.

The three schools were delineated in the 1927-1928 school year. The sports program was expanded, and academic standards were high. Along with English, Polish continued to be spoken and taught.

Recognizing the need for an intellectual, spiritual and cultural center for American Polonia, Orchard Lake founded the Center for Polish Studies and Culture in 1968. Its programs include a Polish Day the first Sunday of each month, an artist-in-residence, a weekly Polish radio Mass, a library of eight thousand Polish books, and the Polish-American archives.

The first Polish-American Heritage Workshop in 1976 focused on all aspects of American Polishness—language, customs, history, folk culture, and theater. The workshop is held at Orchard Lake annually.

The Pope John Paul II Center was established in 1978 to gather, organize and make available material connected with the life, papacy, and teachings of the Polish Pope. It issues newsletters on this subject in English and Polish five times a year.

Pope John Paul II visited Orchard Lake in 1969, before his elevation, and in 1976. He remarked, "If Orchard Lake Schools did not exist, it would be necessary to create them."

Creativity is important at Orchard Lake, where the Polish-born sculptor Marian Owczarski creates his stainless steel works as artist-in-residence. His art, exhibited widely since the early 1960s, is in public and private collections in the United States, Europe, and Canada. A graduate of the Academy of Fine Arts in Warsaw, Owczarski is the master of many media, creating strong, contemporary images. He has worked in the Orchard Lake Schools since 1972.

Orchard Lake Schools offer a unique historical panorama of nearly a hundred carved and costumed figures that move on a narrow conveyor belt from backstage across the stage and then backstage again—all to the accompaniment of a descriptive taped dialogue. The figures include a peasant couple in Poland before written history; Saint Cyril, inventor of the Cyrillic alphabet and translator of the Christian liturgy and Bible into Old Slavonic; Saint Methodius, a Greek Christian bishop possibly active in southern Poland; King Casimir; Tadeusz Kościuszko, who fought in the American Revolution; and many others, including Father Milewski, chancellor of Orchard Lake Schools. The panorama was coordinated by Rev. Zdzislaus Peszkowski, professor of Polish at the seminary, to emphasize the motto of the schools, "For God, Country, and Polonia."

The Orchard Lake Schools Mission Statement: "The mission of the Orchard Lake Schools and Centers, three distinct though related academic institutions and three centers sharing a common Catholic, American, Polish origin and heritage, is to prepare men and women in a Catholic environment for advanced study and/or careers of service. Collectively committed to serve the church within a pluralistic North American cultural context, particularly the Polish American community, the Schools and Centers develop educational, religious, and cultural programs to meet the needs of society."

A few years into its second century, this trinity of schools has educated sixteen thousand students and some three thousand priests for service to God and humankind. The Orchard Lake Schools are the intellectual fountainhead of Polonia, dedicated to keeping alive the traditions and faith of the Polish people, and educating their sons and daughters for a brighter future. Orchard Lake offers a needed and effective opportunity for all who wish to help achieve these goals. It receives and deserves the support of Polish Americans and other Americans.

Old World Wisconsin

The August and Barbara Kruza house of stovewood type construction is displayed at Old World Wisconsin, Eagle, Wisconsin.

Old World Wisconsin, an outdoor museum near Eagle, preserves some of the heritage of the more than 200,000 people of Polish origin who had settled in Wisconsin by 1900.

The August and Barbara Kruza house, for example, has been restored to its 1900 appearance. The house was built in 1884 for the elderly Polish immigrant couple by their son-in-law, Frank Stefaniak, also a Polish immigrant. The house originally stood near Hofa Park, a Shawano County community developed specifically to attract Polish settlers. Frank Stefaniak and his wife, Katharine, lived with their children in the main farm house, while Katharine's parents lived in a smaller house nearby.

Living in a separate residence close to their daughter's home, the Kruzas enjoyed the support and security of their family, yet also had independence and privacy. When the Kruzas needed the family's help, Barbara stepped outside and clanged two tins together. After August died, Barbara continued to live in the house, even though her eyesight was failing. She found her way to the outhouse by following a wire strung to it from the house. Following Polish tradition with its strong emphasis on the family, the Stefaniaks cared for Barbara until she died.

Like most Polish immigrants, the Kruzas brought very little in the way of material wealth to America, but they were hardworking and frugal. The Kruza House shows how an immigrant family with few financial resources adjusted to life in Wisconsin. The house illustrates a building method called stovewood construction. The walls were formed with short, stovewood-length logs set in a bed of mortar, so that the ends of the logs were exposed. This technique was inexpensive and saved labor, allowing one person to construct a building alone. Stovewood buildings were rare in Europe, but they were fairly common in the Hofa Park area. They have been found in areas settled by several ethnic groups in northern Wisconsin, Minnesota, and Canada. Frank Stefaniak blended this New World building technique with an Old World tradition of putting living area and livestock shelter under one roof. The Kruzas lived in the larger portion of the structure. A solid wall separated the living quarters from the smaller area, where Barbara kept chickens. Similar house-barns were common in many European countries and were built by Polish, German, Bohemian, and Finnish immigrants in Wisconsin.

Continued use of the Polish language by the Kruzas and their daughter Katharine helped them maintain cultural ties to their homeland and created a feeling of ethnic identity and community in America. Within three years of arrival, Polish families in Hofa Park had built a small log church. Wayside shrines soon adorned the rural landscape. Churches and schools built by parishes served as community centers. Ethnic bonds, reinforced at church and school, enabled the Kruzas and others to retain a sense of their Polish origins as they gradually developed a new Polish-American identity.

Our Lady of Częstochowa, Queen of Poland

The most venerated painting in the world may be "The Black Madonna of Częstochowa." According to Polish tradition, the image was painted by Saint Luke on a table made by Saint Joseph.

Enshrined at Częstochowa in the south of Poland, the painting of Mother and Child was created in the Helleno-Egyptian iconographic style that goes back to the time of Christ. Its history before 1382 is lost, but tradition holds that Christians flocked to Nazareth after the Resurrection to see the Mother of God, and those who lived too far away earnestly desired her likeness. Thus, Saint Luke was persuaded to paint her portrait.

During the siege of Jerusalem, Christians took the painting with them to a hiding place in the hills, and thereafter it was concealed in underground hideouts and catacombs. In 326 Saint Helena, the mother of Constantine the Great, found the painting in Jerusalem and took it to her son. He installed it in a church at the "hodegetria" or "leader-gate" in Constantinople and chose Mary as Patroness of his New Rome. Her likeness, carried in solemn procession around the city, was credited with scaring off the attacking Saracens. During times of religious persecution the painting was hidden and preserved, remaining in the court of Constantinople for five centuries.

As the Christian faith spread into Europe and Russia, intermarriage among the royalty resulted in the transfer of the precious painting to Belz, which was then in Poland and now is in Ukraine. When the castle of Belz was besieged by the Tatars, a Tatar arrow struck the sacred painting, scarring the throat of the Virgin.

Horrified by the damage, Prince Ladislaus of Opole decided to move the relic to Opole, his birthplace. The way home led through Częstochowa, where he spent the night. In the morning, the cart which carried the sacred picture could not be moved; its wheels were locked. Ladislaus prayed to the Virgin for guidance, and the incident was taken as a sign that the painting should remain in Częstochowa on Jasna Góra (Bright Mountain). The year was 1382.

A church and monastery were erected at Ladislaus's expense, and he brought in from Hungary sixteen monks of the Pauline order to guard the miraculous painting, a responsibility the order has carried out ever since.

The neck scar was not the last damage. A band of Hussites was blamed for two marks made in 1430 on the right cheek of the Virgin's image. All efforts to remove the marks by conservation methods have been unsuccessful.

Why is the painting called the Black Madonna? Some say that smoke from centuries of votive candles darkened the face. Others refer to the verse in the Song of Solomon that says, "I am black but beautiful." Still others reason that Saint Luke saw her as a woman of the eastern Mediterranean, and that if a northern European had painted her, she would have been portrayed as blonde and fair.

The monastery of Jasna Góra was defended against the Swedish army in 1655, and on April 1, 1656, King John Casimir, vowing in prayer in the Cathedral of Lwów, declared the Blessed Virgin as Queen of Poland.

The portrait is draped with many robes made of precious jewels. One robe has been richly beaded with coral by peasant women. At one time, a dress was made of pearls prized for their size and shape, but that gown was stolen in 1909. On Holy Thursday the fathers of the convent take down the painting and carry it into the treasure chamber to change the robes. Then, with prayers and chanting, they carry it back to the sanctuary.

The jeweled gold crowns were given by Pope Pius X to replace the 1717 crown given by Pope Clement XI, which was stolen along with the pearl robe. The first coronation of the Madonna and Child was performed in 1717 before vast crowds of pilgrims. The second was in 1910, attracting a half-million.

The most recent restoration of the painting was done in 1950-51 by Rudolf Kosłowski of Kraków. Henryk Kucharski worked on it in 1945, following the efforts of Jan Rutkowski, head of the art conservation workshop of the National Art Collection in Warsaw, who performed some conservation on it in 1925-1926. There were three early restorations. The first was performed in 1430 after the

OUR LADY OF CZESTOCHOWA. PRAY FOR US.

This outdoor mosaic image of Our Lady of Częstochowa in the Madonna Shrine at St. Stanislaus Church, Milwaukee, Wisconsin, was donated by parishioners as a memorial to the Blessed Coincidence of the Centennial of the Parish and the Millennium of Christianity in Poland in 1966.

Hussite damage. The second was in 1682. A Pauline friar, Makary Sztyftowski, worked on the painting in 1705.

Countless miracles have been attributed to the Black Madonna of Częstochowa. The dead returned to life, the sick were healed, martyrs survived burning at the stake, the raging sea was stilled, madness was replaced by sanity, the blind could see, the condemned were reprieved. No wonder Częstochowa is to the Poles what Lourdes is to the French.

During the Nazi occupation of Poland, dynamite was set to blow up the shrine. A member of the Polish underground, a Franciscan, intercepted the signal for the detonation and cut the wires, saving the Black Madonna for posterity.

Like the early Polish knights who wore images of the Black Madonna on their coats-of-arms, Solidarity leader Lech Wałęsa wears the image on his lapel, and Pope John Paul II has brought it into the Vatican. Polish-American Catholics have erected a chapel to Our Lady of Częstochowa in the crypt of St. Peter's Basilica on Vatican Hill near the tomb of St. Peter.

The people of Poland are strongly disposed to the veneration of Mary in any form, but the Black Madonna is particularly dear to

40

Polish hearts. The first Polish hymn was "Mother of God Virgin," and the Holy See made special provision for an addition to the litany, "Queen of Poland, pray for us," and instituted, for Poland alone, the Feast of the Blessed Virgin Mary, Queen of Poland, on May 3. Today, Poland has 568 churches dedicated to the Mother of God. The Poles credit the 1920 Polish victory over the Russian Bolshevik army to the intercession of Mary.

When Poles left their native land they were given a rosary and an image of the Madonna of Częstochowa to keep them safe. On their lawns they honored Mary with small shrines.

Mary Queen of Poland also reigns in Polish-American hearts. Her chapel in the National Shrine of the Immaculate Conception, Washington, D.C., contains the likeness of Our Lady of Częstochowa painted on wood by Polish artist Leonard Torwit, a replica of the original at Jasna Góra. Polish Americans contributed the marble, mosaics, and tapestries that enrich the shrine. The holy image is framed in gold repousse' and supported by sculpted angels.

The walls of the Washington, D.C., chapel hold the story of Christianity in Poland. The Polish Eagle in white mosaic is suspended in the center of the dome, symbolizing the unconquered spirit of Poland. The chapel was dedicated May 3, 1964, and a pilgrimage sponsored by the Polish Union of America brought Poles from all over the United States to the shrine.

Perhaps the most impressive shrine is at Doylestown, Pennsylvania. A soaring, contemporary church houses a copy of the Black Madonna of Częstochowa. There are two magnificent stained glass windows, one depicting the religious history of the United States and the other the religious history of Poland.

Father Michael M. Zembrzuski dreamed of an American counterpart of the famous Polish shrine, and in 1953 purchased forty acres of land outside Doylestown. He then asked permission to start a monastery and gather some priests and brothers of the Pauline Fathers to help him flesh out the dream. A copy of the miraculous portrait was painted in Poland, touched to the original, and brought to the Pennsylvania chapel created from an old barn. Gradually more land was acquired, adding up to more than 200 acres. Ground-breaking for the new church took place August 23, 1964. John Cardinal Krol, then Archbishop of Philadelphia, was present that day, and two years later, as Poland celebrated one thousand years of Christianity, he dedicated the new Shrine-church to Our Lady of Częstochowa in the presence of guests including President Lyndon B. Johnson and his family.

The shrine is open to the public all through the year. Volunteers for the shrine organize an annual Polish Festival and Country Fair extending from Labor Day weekend through the following weekend, featuring Polish music, dance, food, and games.

October brings the Pułaski Day parade and prayers for Poland on the anniversary of the death of Father Jerzy Popiełuszko. A priest and Solidarity supporter, he held a Mass for Poland each week, and was murdered by security officers.

The Christmas Bazaar opens in late November. Traditional *opłatki* wafers are shared in the shrine cafeteria following the Christmas Eve Mass with its procession to the Christ Child's crib. There's always something Polish happening at Doylestown beneath the benevolent gaze of the Black Madonna of Częstochowa who has witnessed more than a millennium of Polish Christianity.

Another popular Polish shrine is eight miles south of Eureka, Missouri, which is just southwest of St. Louis on Interstate 44. Brother Bronislaus Luszcz, a native of Poland and the founder of the Franciscan Brothers in the United States, devoted twenty-two years to creating this shrine and grotto to Our Lady. Over the chapel altar is a painting of the Black Madonna of Częstochowa by Edward Wroński. The Black Madonna Shrine and Grotto are open daily in spring and summer from 9 a.m. to 7 p.m. Admission is free; a donation is requested for parking.

Another popular pilgrimage for Polish Americans is to the Shrines of the Discalced Carmelites in Munster, Indiana, south of Chicago. From Interstate 80 it is a few blocks south on Highway 41 and a few blocks east. The shrines were built by Carmelite monks who left Poland in 1950 to escape Communist oppression. Founded in the thirteenth century, this religious order has its own revered Madonna, Our Lady Mother of Mercy of Ostra Brama, enshrined at Wilno, where the Carmelites were entrusted with her care in 1671. Special religious events are scheduled every month except January. Polish Masses are said at 9 a.m. and noon every Sunday; English Mass is at 10:30 a.m. There is a dining hall and gift shop.

Greater Love Hath No Man

Father Kolbe

A Polish priest, Father Maximilian Kolbe, a Franciscan, volunteered at Auschwitz to die in place of a man named Franciszek Gajowniczek, who had a family. Father Kolbe was sent to the starvation barracks, where he led his fellow sufferers in prayers and hymns. He survived for so long that the Nazis ended his life with a lethal injection on August 14, 1941.

Father Kolbe was born January 7, 1894, at Zduńska Wola near Łódź and was christened Rajmund. His parents were weavers. The village pharmacist took an interest in Rajmund and tutored him. When Rajmund was attending secondary school at Lwów, the Conventual Franciscans preached a mission, and Rajmund spoke to them about his future. Three years later he joined the Franciscan Order and took the name of Maximilian. He was not happy in the novitiate and thought of leaving, but decided to stay. He studied philosophy at the Gregorian Pontifical Institute in Rome and was ordained a priest April 28, 1918.

While he was in Rome, the Freemasons celebrated their bicentennial and demonstrated against the Church. Father Kolbe decided to mount a defense with the help of the Virgin Mary and founded the Militia of Mary Immaculate.

In 1919 he returned to Poland to teach church history in the seminary at Kraków, but he became ill with tuberculosis and spent nearly two years in a sanatorium at Zakopane.

In the early 1920s the Militia grew so swiftly that communication with all members depended on the printed word. *The Knight of the Immaculate,* a sixteen-page paper, was started. By 1927 its circulation was 60,000.

The same year Father Maximilian founded Niepokalanów (The City of the Immaculate) on land northwest of Warsaw donated by a Polish prince, and built a chapel, dormitory, and printing plant. In 1930 he embarked on an eastern mission to Nagasaki and started a Japanese version of the Militia publication.

Father Kolbe returned to Poland in 1936 to become the superior of Niepokalanów. Prince Drucki-Lubecki had given more land, and the community had grown. By 1938 it was six times its original size, the largest Franciscan monastery in the world.

The German army occupied Niepokalanów in September 1939. Father Kolbe had advised most of the brothers to flee, but he and a few others stayed on. The Germans loaded him and thirty-six others into trucks on September 19. They arrived at Lamsdorf prison September 21 and later were moved to Amtitz. Father Kolbe told the others, "Niepokalanów is wherever its members are. Imprisonment for us is a holy mission."

He was released December 8 and returned to Niepokalanów, to rebuild the ruined complex. Despite sabotage of the presses, he published *The Knight* again. The first, and last, issue appeared in December 1940.

The Gestapo urged him to petition for German citizenship, and when he refused, he was arrested February 17, 1941, and taken to jail in Warsaw. He was transferred to Auschwitz with 320 other prisoners May 28, 1941, and given the identification number 166701. His sufferings and illness there were borne with grace until the end.

In 1963, at the Second Vatican Council, the cardinals and bishops of Poland and Germany submitted a common petition requesting the beatification of Father Maximilian Kolbe. He was canonized at Rome by Pope John Paul II.

In the United States, Father Kolbe, now Saint Maximilian Kolbe, is honored at shrines and chapels and in Polish-American churches. Franciszek Gajowniczek has visited American Polish shrines to tell of his ordeal and of the sacrifice of Saint Maximilian Kolbe.

Pope John Paul II

In the fall of 1978 when the rest of the world was learning to pronounce Wojtyła (voy-TIH-wah), the name of the new pope, Poland needed no instruction. Karol Wojtyła was her own. Elected to the See of Saint Peter, Pope John Paul II wept because he would no longer live in his beloved land.

The fifty-eight-year-old pontiff, the seventh pope of the twentieth century, was the first non-Italian elected since the Dutch Adrian VI (1522-1523). John Paul II was the first pope from the land of the Slavs, the first from a mixed realm of Roman Catholic and Orthodox Christianity, and the first who as a cardinal had to deal with a Communist state and society. He also was the first known actor to become pope.

Called the "Pilgrim Pope," the "Philosopher Pope," the "Poet Pope," and the "People's Pope," John Paul II, even before he took up the papal staff, had visited more of the globe than any previous pontiff.

His countrymen could cite many strengths he would bring to the papacy, including tolerance and defense of liberties without compromising conviction, familiarity with the pluralism of Latin and Byzantine traditions, intense devotion to Mary, and sympathy for the prophetic Polish Messianism of national poets.

Born May 18, 1920, in Wadowice, the second son of his parents, the future pope was christened Carolus Joseph Wojtyła, and was called "Lolek." His boyhood was active, devout, and normal. His mother died in his ninth year. His father, a retired army officer, saw to it that his sons attended Mass regularly, and "Lolek" (the diminutive of Karol) was an altar boy. He also played soccer, hiked, and went skiing and canoeing. Edmund, Karol's brother, became a doctor and died of scarlet fever when Karol was thirteen. Five years later, father and son moved to Kraków.

A neighbor there interested him in acting, which was not difficult in a country that comfortably dramatizes its deepest religious beliefs once a year. Young Karol was deeply imbued with the spirit of the Holy Week. *The Celebration of the Sufferings of the*

Lord and the drama called *The Funeral and Triumph of the Mother of God* are re-enacted annually at the Polish "Oberammergau" by the people of Kalwaria Zebrzydowska and the Franciscan Friars, in thirty tableaus at roadside chapels along five miles of country roads. This deeply moving performance, all within about seven miles of Karol Wojtyła's birthplace, left a lasting and deep impression on him in his youthful years.

He appeared in plays at the Catholic Center and in the high school of Wadowice, and memorized the twelve cantos of the national epic poem *Pan Tadeusz.* Later, he would play a lover, a seer, a king, and Taurus the zodiac bull.

Karol Wojtyła entered Kraków's Jagiellonian University in the fall of 1938 as a student of philosophy and was active in drama that school year. He registered for his second year in the fall of 1939, but World War II intervened. The Nazis invaded Poland September 1, and the teaching staffs went underground.

After his father died of a heart attack in March 1941, Karol Wojtyła moved into a house where a French teacher lived. She taught him French and helped him get a job with the Solvay works, a former Belgian chemical factory with its own quarry. Now he was safe from being transferred to a German factory or detained in a police raid. In his spare time, he acted in underground plays and belonged to a secret prayer group. At one point he was run down by a German truck, injuring the shoulder that is still stooped today.

Always inclined toward piety, he answered the priestly call and began to study under the protection of Metropolitan Adam Sapieha, hero of the Polish Resistance. He worked on his studies at the underground seminary while tending the boiler at the Solvay works.

On Black Sunday, September 7, 1944, when the Nazis made mass arrests, Wojtyła and other seminarians were hidden in the episcopal palace. A friend of those days said of him, "He was bigger than anybody else—not just in size, but in every way."

Karol Wojtyła was ordained a priest on November 1, 1946, and shortly thereafter departed for Rome, where he studied at the Angelicum until June 1948. For his studies, he also went to Louvain in Belgium and to Holland and France.

Father Wojtyła's first parish assignment was in the rural village of Niegowice, Poland, where he went in 1948 and was much loved. A year later, he went to Saint Florian's church in Kraków, and after three years to Saint Catherine's, where he served while studying for his second doctorate.

Refusing pay, he also taught moral philosophy and ethics at Catholic University in Lublin. He took the students on hikes, ski trips, and kayak expeditions, and they called him "Uncle." Father Wojtyła also wrote poetry, including *Quarry*, inspired by his place of work during the German occupation. It begins:

> *Listen: the even knocking of hammers,*
> *So much their own,*
> *I project on to the people*
> *to test the strength of each blow.*

At thirty-eight, Father Wojtyła became Poland's youngest bishop, working sixteen-hour days with an office in the back seat of his car. At forty-three, he became archbishop. He received the cardinal's red hat at forty-seven, becoming the second youngest cardinal in church history.

A model Communist city was being built with no plans for a church, but the people demanded one, and Cardinal Wojtyła helped them in their seven-year fight for a house of worship in Nowa Huta. Given no help by the government, they built the church, in a decade, with their own hands.

Karol Cardinal Wojtyła contributed a great deal, particularly the document on religious freedom, to Vatican II, which changed the face of the Church.

As Pope John Paul II his first ecumenical visit was to Istanbul, Turkey, the home of the Eastern Orthodox Church. Later, he met with the Dalai Lama, the Buddhist leader. He visited the Rome Synagogue to meet Jewish leaders. He also met with Muslim leaders, the Archbishop of Canterbury, and Protestant theologians of central Europe.

John Paul II is the first pope to travel extensively, making apostolic visits to six continents. He has brought messages of consolation and reconciliation, and he has stressed moral and ethical standards among nations. He began his travels with an

Italian pilgrimage to shrines and churches. The following month he visited schoolchildren all over Rome, where police worried about his mingling with the crowds. He ignored their advice, and has never tired of meeting people. Papal audiences tended to be longer than scheduled. He even performed the marriage of the daughter of a street sweeper and a young electrician in February 1979, simply because he met the bride-to-be, and she half-seriously requested it.

Visiting Poland in June 1979, the pope went to his hometowns of Wadowice and Kraków, and prayed at the Auschwitz-Birkenau death camp.

The pope was shot in an assassination attempt on May 13, 1981, in Saint Peter's Square, receiving wounds to the abdomen, arm and hand that required surgery and long convalescence, but he forgave his assailant, a Turkish terrorist, and resumed his world pilgrimages. In 1985, the long trial of Mehmet Ali Agca began. Charges of a Bulgarian conspiracy were dismissed, and Agca was sentenced to life imprisonment. Pope John Paul II has visited him twice in prison and has prayed for him.

The pope has visited the United States four times—in 1979, 1987, 1993, and 1995. The trips have taken him to cities from coast to coast. He met with President Clinton during the two recent visits and in 1995 gave a major address to the United Nations, celebrating its 50th anniversary.

The charismatic pontiff always kneels to kiss the ground of the country he is visiting for the first time, and he smiles broadly when crowds sing the Polish *Sto Lat* (May you live a hundred years). When they chant, "John Paul II, we love you," he responds, "John Paul II, he loves you."

Wherever Pope John Paul II goes, he brings words of encouragement, but he will not waver from the teachings of the Church, particularly those on divorce, abortion, and celibacy of the clergy.

One of his earliest writings (April 9, 1979) dealt with celibacy, affirming the condition that reflects the "purity and perfection of Christ" for the priests of the Church. Even earlier (March 16, 1979) came his encyclical on *The Redeemer of Man*, which calls attention to the welfare of the world's people based on respect for human rights and the sanctity of human life. It deplores social and economic injustice and emphasizes the need to preserve the earth's resources and to control technology.

Pope John Paul II says *I* rather than using the papal *We,* and he's a gregarious man who breakfasts with colleagues and guests before undertaking his heavy daily schedule. Warm and human, but unbending when his principles are assailed, Pope John Paul II truly belongs to the people. He speaks to the whole world, but he has delivered some special messages in his visits to America.

To Polish Americans in 1987 in Hamtramck, Michigan, he said, "Dear brothers and sisters, the more you are aware of your identity, your spirituality, your history, and the Christian culture out of which your ancestors and parents grew, and you yourselves have grown, the more you will be able to serve your country, the more capable will you be of contributing to the common good of the United States."

In 1995, he urged his audiences to attend "to the needs of the poor, the hungry, the homeless, those who are alone or ill."

His message was global during his October 5 visit to the United Nations. The "nonviolent revolutions" that freed his homeland were very much on his mind.

"The revolutions of 1989," the seventy-five-year-old pope said, "were made possible by the commitment of brave men and women inspired by a different, and ultimately more profound and powerful, vision: the vision of man as a creature of intelligence and free will, immersed in a mystery which transcends his own being and endowed with the ability to reflect and the ability to choose—and thus capable of wisdom and virtue...

"We must not be afraid of the future. We must not be afraid of man. It is no accident that we are here. Each and every human person has been created in the image and likeness of the One who is the origin of all that is. We have within us the capacities for wisdom and virtue. With these gifts, and with help of God's grace, we can build in the next century and the next millennium a civilization worthy of the human person, a true culture of freedom. We can and must do so! And in doing so, we shall see that the tears of this century have prepared the ground for a new springtime of the human spirit."

On September 28, 1969, Karol Cardinal Wojtyła of Poland (at right), who later became Pope John Paul II, visited the National Shrine of Our Lady of Częstochowa at Doylestown, Pennyslvania. With him are children and parents, and John Cardinal Krol, archbishop of Philadelphia.

Lech Wałęsa

Lech Wałęsa

Next to Pope John Paul II, Lech Wałęsa is the best-known Pole in the world. He was transformed from an unemployed electrician to the hero of the Gdańsk shipyard strike of August 1980 and the charismatic leader of the trade union Solidarity.

Wałęsa was born September 29, 1943, the son of a village carpenter in Popów. Soon after the birth, the Nazis put his father in a concentration camp, where he died two years later. His widow was left to rear seven children and take care of a seven-acre farm. In 1946, Mrs. Wałęsa married her brother-in-law Stanisław, providing a second father for her children.

Lech was an ordinary boy, playing with toy soldiers and yearning to be a pilot, but he clearly had an influence over his friends and later recalled, "They've always followed me."

Brought up in the Catholic Church, he strayed for two years. One day in a fit of remorse after getting drunk over a girl, he went into a church for shelter from the cold, and, he said, "I felt so good that from that moment I ceased being a layabout." Today, he wears a lapel medallion of Poland's patron saint, the Black Madonna of Częstochowa, and signs important documents with a giant pen that bears the image of the Polish pope.

After three years of secondary school and the obligatory national service, Wałęsa became an electrician near his home village.

He moved to Gdańsk in 1966 and found work in the Lenin shipyard.

Danuta, the pretty florist he courted for a year, became his wife in 1969, and she has provided his serene center through the turbulent years of his activism.

Wałęsa's rise began when he was elected to the strike committee at the shipyard. From the 1970 workers' riots against food price increases and the cost of living, he learned. No one could have controlled the rage of the workers. They took to the streets and were brutally suppressed by the police.

From these events, Wałęsa embraced the wisdom of passive resistance—massive, peaceful, disciplined, and good-humored. A similar strategy had been used by the Polish Communists in the 1920s. Now the day arrived when it would be used against them.

Wałęsa said, "A wall cannot be demolished with butts of the head. We must move slowly, step by step. Otherwise the wall remains untouched, and we break our heads."

Fired by the shipyard in 1976 for protesting poor working conditions, Wałęsa went underground in his struggle for free trade unions. The police detained him hundreds of times, leaving Danuta and their growing number of children in a two-room apartment to wonder what had happened to him. Imprisonment gave him time to think and plan, he said.

By September 1979, Solidarity had created a charter of workers' rights, and Wałęsa was distributing dissident publications near factories, in churches and on public transportation. He operated openly to show the workers they need not fear the authorities, but his activism caused him to lose a number of jobs.

When the peaceful occupation of the Lenin shipyard resulted in victory for the workers, Wałęsa realized the necessity to hold out longer for those in other shipyards who had not yet won their demands.

Becoming a hero of the working class meant more comfortable quarters for the Wałęsa family and broader experience for the head of the household. Wałęsa visited Japan and Italy, conferred with the pope, and won the Nobel Peace Prize in 1983. His face appeared on the cover of *Time* magazine, and he coaxed a one-million-dollar grant from the United States Congress for Solidarity, which was made illegal in 1981 and legalized again in 1989. Although success added to Wałęsa's girth, his Grover Cleveland mustache made him recognizable anywhere in the world.

Wałęsa's supreme victory came in 1990, when he was elected president of Poland. He was, perhaps, the only one who could have unified the Poles then, but the unity was soon shattered. Former Communists, in new democratic parties, gained control of Parliament and the government in 1993. In elections two years later, Wałęsa lost the presidency to Aleksander Kwaśniewski, a former Communist. Kwaśniewski, who speaks English and knows some economics, was considered a modern man, especially by the young people. "Wałęsa is ancient history," said a twenty-year-old student, summing up the attitudes of his generation. Wałęsa, after his electoral defeat, vowed to continue to fight for his vision of a free, democratic Poland.

Wałęsa had a chance to leave Poland years ago. His stepfather asked him to come to New Jersey after his mother died in a car accident (they emigrated in 1973), but Wałęsa spurned what he called "a capitalist existence."

Wałęsa wished to rear his large family in the land of his birth, the land where his voice was the voice of the people. Although he has had detractors, most Poles believe that Lech Wałęsa was the right man at the right time for Poland.

Support for the Homeland

From the Polish American Congress, "Fifty Years Serving the Causes of Polish Americans and the People of Poland."

In May 1944, Polish Americans concerned about whether America's imminent military victory in Europe would bring independence for Poland formed a new political movement—the Polish American Congress.

Since then, three generations of Polish American Congress activists have kept a commitment to the organization's founding principles: support for Poland's right to self-determination, national sovereignty, and reintegration into the democratic family of nations. Equally important is promoting greater knowledge and respect for the Polish cultural heritage in the United States.

The PAC, an "umbrella" organization, is a federation of more than three thousand Polish American organizations and clubs, ranging from national fraternal benefit societies, such as the Polish National Alliance, Polish Women's Alliance, Polish Roman Catholic Union, Polish Falcons, and others, to cultural, professional, religious, veteran, and social associations with total membership of more than a million. PAC by-laws also provide for individual and associate membership. More than fifty PAC divisions and chapters operate in twenty-three states, promoting civic, educational and cultural programs designed to further knowledge about Polish history and culture, and to stimulate Polish-American involvement and recognize accomplishments.

The PAC governing body is the Council of National Directors. Much work is delegated to standing committees, including committees for Polish affairs, American affairs, public affairs, antibigotry, education, Polish American Heritage Month, environmental concerns, and youth.

The organization's record is a proud one. It was one of the first American organizations to warn of the threat to peace posed by the Soviet Union after World War II. It represented the aspirations for freedom and self-determination of the Polish people at the United

Nations, at international conferences, and before United States presidents and Congress. It successfully lobbied for a congressional investigation of the World War II Katyń Forest Massacre, United States backing for Radio Free Europe, international and United States recognition of Poland's post World War II border with Germany, and the admission of several hundred thousand Polish refugees to the United States in the years after World War II, in the 1950s, and in the 1980s.

In the 1990s, PAC leaders met with top leaders including President Bill Clinton and Vice President Albert Gore to urge them to support NATO membership for Poland, the Czech Republic, Hungary and Slovakia.

Since the collapse of communism in Eastern Europe, the PAC has promoted American investment in Poland; monitored legislation on immigration reform and other domestic issues affecting Polish Americans; opened cultural, religious and political dialogues with other ethnic groups in the United States; supported educational and cultural activities in the Polish-American community; sponsored visits to the United States of representatives of the Polish government and people; supported the appointment of Polish Americans to high positions in government; and initiated designation of October as Polish American Heritage Month.

The PAC established its Charitable Foundation in 1971 to support cultural, educational and humanitarian activities that emphasize the Polish-American heritage.

In 1981, the foundation initiated the Relief for Poland project at the request of Lech Wałęsa, the first democratically elected president of Poland, and the Polish Episcopate Charity Commission. Since then, the foundation has sent to Poland countless shipments of medicines, hospital equipment, medical supplies, rehabilitation equipment and children's vitamins. Thanks to individual and corporate donors, the foundation in thirteen years sent more than $200 million worth of humanitarian aid, at a cost of just over $10 million.

The Immortal Chopin

Frédéric François Chopin, whose music has been called "the finest art Poland ever produced," was born in 1810 in the village of Żelazowa Wola west of Warsaw. His birthplace is now a museum dedicated to his memory.

This house was the home of the Skarbeks, who employed Chopin's father Nicholas, a professor of French, as a tutor for their children. Nicholas Chopin was born in eastern France in a village belonging to a Polish nobleman. At age sixteen

Frédéric Chopin

Nicholas traveled to Poland in the nobleman's service and chose to stay to avoid conscription into the French army.

While tutoring for the Skarbeks he met Justyna, a Polish lady-in-waiting who played the piano well. They married in 1806 and had four children, including Frédéric.

The young Chopin was sensitive and poetic as he grew up in Warsaw, where the family moved shortly after his birth. His passion for music started early, and at age seven he began piano lessons with Adalbert Zywny, a Bohemian composer. Chopin preferred improvisation to straight practicing of his lessons.

In the fall of 1823 he entered the Warsaw *Liceum*. Two years later, he played for the Tsar and published his first written work, *Rondo in C minor*. He enrolled at the Warsaw Conservatory in 1826. His first nocturne, a form he made uniquely his own, was composed in 1827. In 1828 Chopin went to Berlin, where he met Felix Mendelssohn, only one year his senior. In 1829 he went to Vienna. The Viennese loved his *Chmiel* theme from a Polish drinking song, but in general they didn't care for his reserved and delicate style of playing. Chopin returned to Warsaw and completed his *Piano Concerto in F minor* in 1830, the year he fell in love with the Polish soprano Konstancja Gładkowska. She did not return his passion.

Chopin left Warsaw November 2, 1830, with a premonition that he would never return. Several weeks later the November Uprising led to revolution against the Tsar. Poland, which had been "divided up" by Russia, Austria, and Prussia in the partitions of 1772, 1793, and 1795, came under even more oppressive treatment, and Chopin never went home again. He settled in Paris, not realizing that he was in his father's native land, and joined the Paris intellectuals who called themselves "Children of the Century."

For a time Chopin could not decide whether he wanted to be a pianist or a composer. He decided that the strenuous life of a virtuoso was not for him. Members of the rich Rothschild banking family became his patrons, and this prestige attracted piano pupils. Chopin became rich on five lessons a day, and publishers became interested in his compositions.

Chopin had explored the melodies and meters of national dances such as the *krakowiak*, the *mazurka*, and the *polonaise*. In 1834 Adam Mickiewicz's *Pan Tadeusz* was published and became the Polish national epic, evoking an atmosphere that Chopin captured in his music.

Chopin met George Sand (Aurore Dupin Dudevant), the French novelist, in 1836, and they became lovers two years later in Majorca. He spent years at her country house at Nohant, and his final works were composed there. Sand's novel *Lucrezia Floriani*, published in 1846, was based on their relationship. Complicated domestic difficulties involving Sand's children led to a complete break between the two. Chopin left, and never composed again.

He played concerts in England and Scotland. Proceeds of his last concert were given to aid Polish refugees. Suffering from consumption, he returned to France. He died in 1849. Absent from his native land for the last nineteen years of his life, he carried Poland in his heart and put the soul of Poland into his music. The world is a happier place because of Chopin's delightful music.

Crazy Horse Memorial photo

"Paderewski: Study of an Immortal," a marble portrait by Polish-American sculptor Korczak Ziolkowski was voted best sculpture at the New York World's Fair in 1939. The twice-life-size sculpture weighs 1,200 pounds and was carved in 1935.

Paderewski: Pianist, Patriot

The name "Paderewski" has symbolized classical music for generations of Americans, and the great virtuoso also was the inspiration for Polish independence after World War I.

Born in 1860 in Kuryłówka, Podolia (now in Ukraine), Ignacy Jan Paderewski showed talent early, studied first at the Warsaw Music Institute (where he was briefly ousted for insubordination), later in Berlin, and under the great pianist Theodor Leschetitzky (born Leszetycki) in Vienna. His debut in Vienna in 1887 was a huge success. Following his New York debut in 1891, he made 108 appearances in 112 days in the United States, and performed all over the world to unprecedented acclaim.

After his concerts, the tall and handsome Paderewski was approached on the stage by crowds, mostly young women. Some sought merely to touch the great artist, others wanted a lock of hair or a piece of clothing as a souvenir. In 1892 he made a second American tour, traveling in his own railroad car with a piano so he could practice while the train was moving.

Paderewski had married in 1880. His bride died in childbirth the following year. At the turn of the century, Paderewski lived in Switzerland and his name, along with the names of glamorous women with whom he had been seen, appeared regularly in the gossip columns. He did not marry any of these women. His second wife was the former Helena Górska, a friend from his student days. She had cared for his son, who was crippled and in a wheelchair, and eventually divorced her first husband to marry Paderewski.

His first published composition was *Impromptu in F* in 1879, but his signature for all time is the *Minuet in G*. His other compositions, including *Symphony in B minor*, won a hearing primarily because of Paderewski's keyboard brilliance. His opera *Manru* premiered in Dresden and was staged by the New York Metropolitan Opera in 1902 before touring to Philadelphia, Boston, Pittsburgh, Chicago, and Baltimore.

In 1909 Paderewski became director of the Warsaw Music Institute, but in 1914 at the start of World War I, he settled temporarily in Paso Robles, California. During the war he donated all income from his public appearances to Polish war victims and led the movement to make Poland independent after more than a century of subjugation. In January 1919, Paderewski became Poland's first premier and foreign minister. He was a signer of the Versailles Treaty in June 1919.

The artist had difficulty, however, in working with politicians and politics, and was discouraged by the failure to achieve national unity. He resigned in November 1919 and resumed his concert tours two years later.

When the Germans invaded Poland in 1939, Paderewski joined the Polish government-in-exile in France and was president of its parliament during 1940. He returned to the United States

In the Paderewski room of the Polish Museum of America in Chicago, Adela Zydel holds orthopedic shoes made for Paderewski by her father, Piotr Wasiewicz. She donated the shoes to the museum.

late that year and worked for the Allied cause until his death in New York in June 1941. He was buried in Arlington National Cemetery in Washington, D.C., as the only non-United States citizen there. After the war, his remains were moved to Wawel Castle in Kraków. His huge library and archives and a large sum of money went to the Jagiellonian University in Kraków.

Paderewski is remembered as a man of striking appearance, personal magnetism, and artistic temperament who earned a great fortune with his art and dispensed it generously. He gave $50,000 to Chopin Memorial Hall in Warsaw and $100,000 toward the giant memorial statue of King Władysław Jagiełło in Kraków. His playing was poetic and idiosyncratic. He made many recordings for mechanical pianos and phonographs, and played the piano in the 1936 English film, *Moonlight Sonata*.

Madame Curie

Maria Skłodowska, born November 7, 1867, in Warsaw, was an exceptional child who could read at the age of four and was destined for world fame as Marie Curie, the discoverer of radium.

Madame Curie

Her father, Władysław Skłodowski, taught mathematics and physics in a high school. His workroom was filled with physics apparatus that fascinated Maria, the youngest of his five children.

Maria graduated from the Gymnasium on June 12, 1883, with a gold medal, and spent an idyllic year in the country contemplating her future.

She returned to Warsaw and the unrewarding job of tutoring lazy pupils whose parents frequently forgot to pay. Still, she saved money from her meager earnings to help support the medical studies of her sister, Bronia, in Paris.

Maria became a governess, leaving her first impossible post for a happier situation in the country. Kazimierz, the eldest son of that household, fell in love with her and she with him, but the family objected to the match. Despite this humiliation, she stayed on. Her sister in Paris depended on her.

In the spring of 1889, she found another position in Warsaw and went home to live with her father. A cousin, Józef Boguski, was the director of the Museum of Industry and Agriculture with a secret laboratory within its walls, and it was here that Maria's love affair with science really began.

She went to Paris in 1891 to live with Bronia and her new

husband and to study at the Sorbonne, but their domestic life was too pleasurably distracting. Now known as Marie, she took a series of wretched rooms near the Sorbonne, plunging into her studies, subsisting on tea and buttered bread and sometimes fainting from malnutrition and exhaustion. After earning a degree in physics in 1893, she earned another in mathematics the following year.

Considering the disastrous experience with Kazimierz, Marie had abandoned all thoughts of love, but when she met Pierre Curie, a scientist whose passion for the discipline matched her own, she changed her mind. They were married in 1895. Two years later, Marie gave birth to their daughter, Irène. Their second daughter, Eve, was born in 1904.

Marie Curie became interested in the uranium experiments of Henri Becquerel and began to explore the phenomenon of radiation. The Curies spent four miserable but glorious years in an unheated shed with a leaking roof breaking down pitchblende ore in search of a new element, and they found two. Marie named the first *polonium* in honor of her native country, and the second was *radium*. The year was 1898. The Curies and Henri Becquerel shared the 1903 Nobel prize in physics for the discovery of radioactivity. That word was first used in 1898 by Marie Curie.

Pierre Curie died beneath the wheels of a horse-drawn wagon in April 1906. Despite her grief, Madame Curie continued her research and was awarded the 1911 Nobel Prize in chemistry for the discovery of polonium and radium.

She held no patent on her discoveries and wished for none, saying, "Radium belongs to the people." One of her great satisfactions was its use to arrest cancer, and the treatment was named Curietherapy in her honor.

During World War I, Marie Curie organized radiological cars to X-ray the war wounded. She was the first technician and trained others.

She was given her late husband's chair at the Sorbonne, was elected to the French Academy of Medicine, and had the satisfaction of laying the cornerstone for the Radium Institute of Warsaw.

In 1921 Marie Curie, accompanied by her two daughters, made a triumphant visit to the United States and was given a gram of radium purchased with funds donated by American women. The presentation was by President Warren Harding.

Untouched by fame, Marie Skłodowska-Curie put science first in her life, but her long and continued exposure to the element she discovered enabled it to attack her bone marrow. She died in July, 1934, assured of a kind of immortality she cared nothing about. A lifetime of unrelenting research meant more to her than being called the mother of the atomic age.

After formal education, Marie Curie's daughter Irène became her mother's assistant in 1918, and in 1925 Frédéric Joliot became an assistant. They were married in 1926, and both devoted themselves to carrying on Marie Curie's work through intensive research in areas related to nuclear fission, biology, and medicine. The Joliot-Curies were awarded the 1935 Nobel Prize in chemistry for discovery of artificial radioactive elements.

As early as 1903 Pierre Curie had warned of the dangers of radioactivity "in criminal hands." With the rise of Nazi Germany, the Joliot-Curies in 1939 abandoned their practice of open publication of research results. They sealed their writings on nuclear reactors. Frédéric hid a stockpile of uranium, and arranged for the world stockpile of heavy water (140 quarts) to be moved from Norway to France and later to England.

Irène Joliot-Curie died in 1956 of leukemia resulting from the same long exposure that had taken her mother. Frédéric Joliot-Curie died in 1958.

Saving Mankind

Dr. Albert B. Sabin

The polio epidemics that frightened generations of parents in the first half of this century are a fading memory, thanks in part to a Polish-born scientist.

School children since 1960 have been protected from the dreaded disease by a live polio vaccine first developed by Dr. Albert B. Sabin, who was born in 1906 in Białystok, Poland.

In 1921, the Sabin family of six, including four children, came to the United States and settled in Paterson, New Jersey. Young Albert joined literary and debating societies at Paterson High School and graduated in 1923. He worked at odd jobs to get money for college and graduated from New York University in 1928. He promptly entered the university's college of medicine, was a Bullowa Scholar doing research on various types of pneumonia and got his medical degree in 1931. During his internship at Bellevue Hospital in New York, he isolated Virus B, a virus found in monkeys, and decided to devote his career to medical research.

After a year of postgraduate study at the Lister Insitute of Preventive Medicine in London, England, he joined the staff of the Rockefeller Institute of Medical Research. In 1939, he accepted an appointment as associate professor of pediatrics at the University of Cincinnati College of Medicine and as a fellow of its Children's Hospital Research Foundation.

In the U.S. Army Medical Corps during World War II, Sabin's projects included development of a vaccine against dengue fever and the successful vaccination of sixty-five thousand military personnel on Okinawa against Japanese encephalitis. He had developed the vaccine in1942 at the Children's Hospital in Cincinnati.

After the war, Sabin returned to Cincinnati as a professor of research pediatrics and turned his attention to poliomyelitis. His focus was on development of a vaccine that used weakened live polio viruses, a technique used in developing vaccines for smallpox and yellow fever. Meanwhile, Dr. Jonas Salk was developing

64

a dead-virus vaccine. The Salk vaccine was approved first, but Sabin continued his work. He believed a live-virus vaccine would afford immunity over a longer period of time, perhaps for life.

Sabin tried his vaccine first on chimpanzees. In 1955, he began inoculating prisoner volunteers at the federal reformatory in Chillicothe, Ohio, with inoculations for each of the three types of polio viruses. The testing continued until 1960, using volunteers and others in seven countries around the world.

Benefits claimed for the Sabin vaccine, in addition to its promise of lifetime immunity, were that it could be taken orally, stored indefinitely in deepfreeze units and produced cheaply. After the vaccine's approval in 1960, school children across the country lined up to take the polio vaccine in sugar cubes.

Sabin spent his life studying viruses of all kinds. His later research focused on the relationship between viruses and cancer. He died March 3, 1993.

Sabin won many honors during his lifetime, including forty honorary degrees from universities around the world, the Presidential Medal of Freedom in 1986, the Order of Friendship Among Peoples from the Union of Soviet Socialist Republics in 1986, the Distinquished Civilian Service Medal from the United States Army in 1973, the Gold Medal from the Royal Society of Health in London in 1969, the Albert Lasker clinical medical research award in 1965, and the Antonio Feltrinelli prize in medical and surgical science from the Academia Nazionale dei Lincei in Rome in 1964.

Joseph Rotblat

Joseph Rotblat, a physicist born in Poland, won the 1995 Nobel Peace Prize for his forty-year campaign against nuclear weapons.

Rotblat helped build the world's first atomic bomb in the United States during World War II, but he quit the project in 1944 when he overheard a U.S. general say its real purpose was to subdue the Soviet Union, not Nazi Germany. He was the only scientist to quit.

He switched from nuclear physics to medical physics, moved to Great Britain and joined forces with Albert Einstein, Bertrand Russell and other scientists in a campaign against nuclear weapons. The scientists have sponsored hundreds of Pugwash Conferences over the years to focus on the issue.

Celebrities

Glamorous women, strong men, and extraordinary talents among Polish Americans account for many of the stars of American entertainment and sports.

Polish women of outstanding allure became the idols of the stage and screen. Pola Negri was Apolonia Chałupiec before she played opposite Rudolph Valentino and introduced painted toenails.

Gloria Swanson's parents were wealthy landowners in the Austrian part of partitioned Poland. She took Hollywood by storm.

Broadway dancer Gilda Grey was Maryanna Michalska before she popularized the shimmy and the black bottom and became a star of the Ziegfeld Follies.

Estelle Clark, a Hollywood actress of the 1920s, was born Stasia Zwolińska. Carole Landis, famous for her beauty and movies like *One Million B.C.* with Victor Mature, was of Polish descent. So was Jean Wallace, a Paramount actress who changed her name from Janina Walasek and married Franchot Tone.

Carol Baker (Karolina Piekarska) starred in the film *Baby Doll.* Loretta Swit of *M*A*S*H,* the long-running television show, is known to Americans as "Hot Lips," the character she played. Stephanie Powers (Stefania Federkiewicz) acts in stage, film, and television productions.

Martha Stewart (Martha Kostyra) gives tips for fine dining, decorating and entertaining on her how-to television show and in her magazine, both aptly named "Martha Stewart Living." Her eleven books have sold more than 2.8 million copies.

Jack Palance, formerly Walter Palaniuk, is a veteran of screen, stage, and television. Charles Bronson (Buchinski) has starred on television and in many movies. Michael Landon, whose name was Orowicz, won fame in *Bonanza, Little House on the Prairie* and other television series.

Polish-born film-maker Roman Polanski created movies such as *Rosemary's Baby*, a tale of the occult. Krzysztof Komeda of Poland (1931-1969) wrote the lullaby music for the film.

Joseph Mankiewicz has been producing motion pictures for decades, and Bronisław Kaper has written musical scores for films and light classics.

Stars of Sports

In the world of sports, Stanley Ketchel (Stanisław Kiecal) became middleweight boxing champion of the world in 1908. Tony Zale (Antoni Zaleski) won the middleweight championship in 1940.

Stanislaw "Zbyszko" Cyganiewicz became world wrestling champion in 1921. The most popular sports figure in the United States in the early twenties, he was a philosophy graduate of the University of Vienna and spoke eleven languages.

Stella Walsh (Stanisława Wałasiewicz) was barred from representing the United States in the 1932 Olympic Games because she was not born in America. She competed for Poland and won a gold medal in the hundred-meter dash.

Another Polish-American Olympian is Janet Lynn (Nowicki), who won five gold medals in figure-skating before going professional as an Ice Follies star.

In football, the memorable Polish names begin with that of Frank Piekarski, the first Polish American to join the All-American football squad of 1904. Bronisław "Bronko" Nagurski, an All American at the University of Minnesota in the 1920s, led the Chicago Bears to three National Football League titles and is in college and professional halls of fame. Succeeding football standouts have included John Matuszak of the Washington Redskins and the Oakland Raiders, Ed Modzelewski of the New York Giants, Walt Patulski of Notre Dame and the St. Louis Cardinals, Greg Landry of the Detroit Lions, Ron Jaworski of the Los Angeles Rams, Mark Olejniczak of the New York Giants, Bob Bobrowski of the Baltimore Colts, Danny Abramowicz of the San Francisco Forty-niners, and Steve Okoniewski and Chester Marcol of the Green Bay Packers.

Baseball greats Stan Musial of the St. Louis Cardinals and Carl "Yaz" Yastrzemski of the Boston Red Sox are household words in this country. Other Polish-American stalwarts of the sport include Steve Gromek, Ray Jablonski, Ted Kazanski, Ted Kluszewski, Jim Konstanty, Tony Kubek, Bob Kuzava, Chet Laske, Ed Lopat, Eddie

Lubanski, Greg Luzinski, Hank Majeski, Cass Michaels, Pete Rose, George Shuba, Al Simmons, Bill Skowron, and Richie Zisk.

Many Polish-American celebrities changed their names for the sake of pronounceability, but Knute Rockne, coach of Notre Dame's Fighting Irish in the 1920s, used to say, "If I can't pronounce their names, I know they're good."

Drawing by Alice Wadowski-Bak

Poles love the dramatic and spiritual expression in their carolers who go from home to home singing kolędy. *In villages, young men called star carriers held a long pole with an illuminated star on top. The star could spin, and often had a nativity scene. The person carrying the animal head is called the* turon *and does comical tricks, a practice dating from pagan times. Some carolers put on puppet shows.*

Folk Music and Dance

Despite the dramatic contrast between Chopin's *Fantasia on Polish Airs for Piano and Orchestra* and Ed Krolikowski's *Baruska Polka*, or between the stately polonaise of the Polish court and the Polish-American polka, they all stem from the same vital source, the Polish spirit.

Chopin was deeply influenced by the rhythms of music for Polish folk dances. The polonaise is a processional dance of striding steps with the accent on the first beat of the measure. Originally, it was danced only by men, as a receiving line for leaders of ancient tribes. The polonaise came to court, perhaps as early as 1573, becoming a partnered procession of people lined up according to rank. This elegant dance became the traditional opening of formal events. Today it's an important part of the Legion of Young Polish Women's annual White and Red Ball, the presentation of Polish-American debutantes in Chicago, with proceeds of the event funding Polish causes. That ball also includes the mazurka, a fiery, emotional dance that originated in central Poland.

The *kujawiak* is danced in three-quarter time with romantic, easy motion, and the *oberek* is a group dance that involves stamping feet, shouts, and fast whirling. Occasionally couples will break from the group to perform lifts, kicks, or cartwheels in the air.

The *krakowiak*, which originated in Kraków, is a syncopated dance in 2/4 time that is the most widely recognized dance of Poland. Exuberant and energetic, it involves stamping, kicks, cries, and leaps, and usually is accompanied by song.

The Highlanders of the Tatra mountain region are some of the best and most unusual dancers in Poland. The *taniec góralski* (Highlanders' dance) involves men and women performing separately with the men trying to impress the women. A male dancer may choose a partner, sending a friend to make the approach.

Highlanders and bagpipes suggest Scotland to some Americans, but not to Polish Americans. Five types of bagpipes have been in use in Poland for generations, and the Highlanders, whose music and rhythms are fast, live in the mountains where southern Poland meets Slovakia. During the Prussian partition of Poland in the nineteenth century, the use of bagpipes was banned by the German occupation forces as symbols of the stubborn, undying Polish spirit.

Violins, the "highlander bassoon," assorted bagpipes (*kobza* and *dudy*), and the *gęśle*, a four-stringed instrument, provide the music for most Polish folk dancing.

Costumes for Polish folk dances reflect the colorful styles of the many regions that gave birth to the dances. Bright sashes, rich brocades, velvets, heavy embroidery, satin, embroidered tulle, and red leather boots give the dancers a dazzling appearance.

Poland has two professional folk ensembles, *Mazowsze*, founded in 1949, and *Śląsk*, established in 1953. Both have stylized the national dances, but their verve and showmanship have done much to promote Poland's folk culture throughout the world.

In America, Polish fraternal insurance companies sponsor many folk dancing classes and groups. To finance their costumes, the *Echo Polonii Tancerze* dancers of Niagara Falls, New York, have an "Adopt a Dancer" program. Marilyn Herowski of the Echo Society founded this dance group in 1981. Costumes come from Katowice in Silesia. The dancers have performed in New York state and Canada and at Walt Disney World in Florida.

Polish-American dancers at the International Dance Festival in 1974 in Rzeszow, Poland, decided that the United States also should have folk dance festivals. Annual events, at first sponsored by the American Council of Polish Cultural Clubs, began in 1978, with some festivals in the United States and some in Poland. Participants organized as the Polish Folk Dance Association of the Americas in 1983. The association's North American festivals continue to bring knowledge of the beauty and richness of Polish folklore to younger generations of Polish Americans.

The polka originated in Czechoslovakia in 1830, and after a "polkamania" in Paris and London in 1844, it became popular throughout Europe and the Americas. But Poles had little connection with it until they came to America. Polka researchers Charles and Angela Keil of Buffalo, New York, and Dick Blau of Milwaukee note that hundreds of thousands of Polish Americans have been following their favorite polka bands since the 1920s. Two styles prevail: Eastern and Chicago.

During the 1940s and 1950s, big bands in Buffalo and the East mixed polkas, obereks, waltzes, and swing to the delight of huge crowds. "It was a golden era and one of fine musicianship," the polka researchers wrote. "Almost everyone read music, arrangements were tricky, tempos were brisk, and bands were admired for the crisp articulation of the saxophone section, impossibly difficult clarinet duets, and perfect unison from triple-tonguing trumpet players." The last great Eastern band, the Connecticut Twins, Jaś and Staś, perfected the style, providing the model for other Eastern bands in the 1950s.

By this time, Li'l Wally Jagiello was getting his act together in Chicago. His style was slow tempos, loose phrasing, a whining squeezebox concertina, and unembarrassed vocals "from the heart." Li'l Wally was a one-man band, hitting the bass drum with his foot, squeezing the concertina, and singing. At first, his records were rejected by disc jockeys, but the people liked what they heard and demanded his music. His musical idiom spoke to some deep memory of the Galicia area of Poland.

Today some cities with large Polish-American populations have polka programming all day on one radio station or another. Radio polka music has been big since the late 1920s, when Polish Americans in Bridgeport, Connecticut, asked Ed Królikowski to line up sponsors and do a radio broadcast.

Challenged to do something Polish and American that would appeal to all Americans, Królikowski drew on his Dixieland jazz and vaudeville experience. One of his first records was "The Baruska Polka," which became the 1950s hit tune "She's Too Fat for Me." Bands in Hartford, Connecticut; Springfield, Massachusetts; and Chicago were broadcasting and recording, and the polka took off as "Polish American" music.

Tempos speeded up and arrangements became more complex in the big bands of Walt Solek, Frank Wojnarowski, Ray Henry, Gene Wiśniewski, and Bernie Witkowski.

After World War II Antonia Błazończyk presented the music of her southern Poland ancestors, the Highlanders, in Chicago's Pułaski Ballroom. Polka music was played five nights a week, and

71

Eddie Błazończyk and his Versatones

Antonia's son Eddie played the accordion and performed ethnic dances. In his youth, Eddie Błazończyk hit the rock concert circuit as Eddie Bell and the Hill Boppers. Later, he won the National Academy of Recording Artists Grammy twice for his Polish-American polka albums. He still tours with Eddie Błazończyk's Versatones.

Today polka fans charter buses to attend the concerts of their favorite polka bands and book polka cruises several years in advance. There is even a Polka Music Hall of Fame in Chicago, sponsored by the International Polka Association. Leon Kozicki, the first president of the association, said more than half of those honored were leaders of Polish-American polka bands.

The very first polka party may have been a wedding, still a fine occasion for this special music and dancing. All ages participate, and everybody dances. There's a wide tolerance for different styles of clothing, hair, and demeanor, according to polka researchers Blau and the Keils, and musicians are expected to be "part of the crowd and play until they're exhausted." Guests are expected to "drink a lot (eat some, too) to get silly or happy but not to get drunk, and there should be no fights."

It's absolutely necessary that everybody has a good time.

*Adult dancers in the Polonia Song and Dance Company
of Pittsburgh, Pennsylvania*

Young people in the Polonia Song and Dance Company

The Polish Love of Words

From the twelfth-century *Chronicles of Gallus* to the late twentieth-century survival novels of Polish-born author Jerzy Kosinski, Polish literature has been passionate. Despite the frequent and devastating disruptions of the Polish nation, the literature has developed steadily, sharing all the great religious, intellectual and cultural movements of the West.

Adopting Christianity from Rome turned Poland's face westward, a betrayal in the eyes of their Russian neighbors but a more civilized choice in the view of western European Catholics. The first writings were religious and in Latin. Jan Długosz wrote the first extensive history of Poland in Latin in the fifteenth century. Nicolaus Copernicus (1473-1543), the astronomer who discovered that the earth revolves around the sun, also wrote in Latin.

A Hymn to the Mother of God (Bogurodzica) is the earliest piece of vernacular literature. Mikołaj Rey's *A Short Discourse Among the Squire, the Bailiff and the Parson,* an earthy satire on contemporary social and religious conditions, was written in Polish and published in 1543, a date considered to be the beginning of modern Polish literature.

The foremost writer of Renaissance Poland was Jan Kochanowski (1530-1584), who wrote a poetic cycle in the sixteenth century in memory of his young daughter Urszula. His work laid the groundwork for future Polish theater.

The Poles, a dramatic people, understand and respond to the deeply moving events of Holy Week and the Christian story staged annually at Kalwaria Zebrzydowska.

Polish language and style were influenced by the 1599 translation of the Bible by Jakub Wujek, a Jesuit. Piotr Skarga (1536-1612), the most outstanding preacher of old Poland, wrote *Diet Sermons* condemning abuses by the gentry class and hardships visited upon the peasants. Szymon Symonowicz (1558-1629) wrote Latin poems and Polish tales of country life. Maciej Sarbiewski (1595-1640) wrote *Latin Odes* that won him the title, "the Christian Horace," but the enlivening spirit of Humanism was waning.

Literature turned traditionally Polish, changing from classic to baroque spiced with Latin. Wacław Potocki (1625-1696) wrote historical epics celebrating the repelling of the Turks by the Poles and Cossacks.

Seventeenth-century prose consisted of diaries, journals, and memoirs. In his famous *Memoirs*, which reads like a novel, Jan Chryzostom Pasek (1636-1701) anticipated Sir Walter Scott.

The first half of the eighteenth century (the reign of the Saxon kings) was known as the "Saxon Night," a time of political decay and intellectual stagnation. Two women writers of the period chose vastly different subject matter. Elżbieta Drużbacka (1695-1765) wrote of sensual love, and Konstancja Benisławska, a noblewoman from Livonia, wrote religious poems.

A renaissance of Polish culture occurred in the reign of Stanisław II August Poniatowski, the last king of Poland, who ruled from 1764 to 1795. Ignacy Krasicki (1735-1801) wrote the first modern Polish novel, *The Adventures of Nicholas Doświadczyński*.

Julian Ursyn Niemcewicz (1757-1841), a prolific writer, went to the United States, where he became a friend of Thomas Jefferson and wrote an extensive diary describing the country just after the American Revolution. His memoirs include a lively description of the beauty of the mighty falls at Niagara.

The fall of the Polish state at the end of the eighteenth century coincided with the flowering of Polish romantic poetry. Adam Mickiewicz (1798-1855) wrote his famous *Ode to Youth* in 1820, heralding the dawn of liberty. Exiled to Russia, he continued to write and won the admiration of Alexander Pushkin, the great Russian poet. Mickiewicz's greatest claim to fame is *Pan Tadeusz* (1834), the first great national epic in Polish literature. It is set in Lithuania on the eve of Napoleon's invasion of Russia in 1812.

Juliusz Słowacki (1809-1849), a rival of Mickiewicz, was greatly influenced by Shakespeare. He wrote plays in diverse styles, including *Mazeppa* (1839), the story of a European Buffalo Bill. Zygmunt Krasinski (1812-1859) wrote *The Undivine Comedy*, foretelling a revolution a century in the future. Cyprian K. Norwid (1821-1883) continued the tradition of Romantic philosophy. His play *Cleopatra* is a psychological drama.

After the second tragic insurrection against the Russian Tsarist government in 1863, writers gave up the Romantic dream and opted for Positivism. They extolled the virtue of work and examined the sober realities of Poland's economic and social life. Józef I. Kraszewski (1812-1887), a historical author, wrote hundreds of novels, poems, essays, dramas, and treatises in this period, pioneering in fiction. The most eloquent representative of Positivism was Bolesław Prus (pseudonym of Alexander Głowacki, 1845-1912), who wrote *The Doll*, depicting the social strata of Warsaw.

Henryk Sienkiewicz (1846-1912) was the best known Polish author and won the 1905 Nobel Prize for his historical novels, including *Quo Vadis*. He was sent to Philadelphia to cover the Centennial Exposition in 1876 and searched for a California site for communal living. At Anaheim he found Helena Modrzejewska, the actress known as "the great Modjeska," but the communal idea was short-lived.

Eliza Orzeszkowa (1841-1910) wrote stories and novels about Jews and peasants. She reproached Joseph Conrad for forsaking his native tongue. He, in turn, called her "that hag." Conrad was born in the Ukraine in 1857. His full name was Teodor Józef Konrad Nałęcz Korzeniowski. His father was deported to northern Russia in 1862, and the family went with him. The parents died, leaving the youth with his mother's relatives. He was an avid reader in French and Polish, and just before his seventeenth birthday, he left Poland for France and the sea. His experiences and reflections resulted in a number of classic novels in English, including *Lord Jim, Heart of Darkness*, and *Nostromo*—major contributions to modern literature. He died in 1924.

Gabriela Zapolska (1857-1921) was an actress, playwright and novelist whose play *Mrs. Dulska's Morality* is still in Polish theatrical repertoires. Stanisław Wyspiański (1869-1907), a playwright, painter, and poet, gave the Polish theater new vision with his Greek tragedies. His play *The Wedding* (1901) used a puppet theater technique to criticize Polish society.

In the late nineteenth century, reaction against Positivism became the Young Poland movement. Lyric poetry, the novel, and drama flourished. Stefan Żeromski (1864-1925) created a new form of the novel, lacing realistic devices with lyricism.

Władysław Reymont (1867-1925) wrote the four-volume novel

The Peasants, which earned him fame that culminated in the 1924 Nobel Prize for literature.

Tadeusz (Boy) Żeleński, who founded the literary cafe Little Green Balloon, wrote cabaret scripts in everyday language and became a first-rate critic and translator. Bolesław Leśmian (1878-1937), called "the poet's poet," is considered a major twentieth-century Polish poet.

After World War I, a new generation of lyric poets started the Skamander movement, named for the river on which Troy stood. The most outstanding was Julian Tuwim (1894-1953), who has been called "the Polish Walt Whitman." Kazimierz Wierzyński, one of the founders of Skamander, is remembered for his eulogy of sport, *The Olympic Laurel.*

The Theater of the Absurd made its debut in Poland at least twenty years before Beckett, Ionesco, and Genet presented it as something new. The absurdist playwright was Stanisław Witkiewicz (1885-1939), whose work has some of the flavor of the American 1960s. *The Madman and the Nun,* a short play created in 1923, has been translated into English and represents the themes and techniques in all Witkiewicz's plays.

Realism marked the novels of the post-World War I period. Zofia Nałkowska (1885-1954) explored the feminine psyche, and Maria Dąbrowska's masterpiece is *Nights and Days* (1932-1934), a four-volume epic of everyday life.

In the late twenties and thirties, Polish novelists were in close touch with European literature. Joseph Wittlin's *Salt of the Earth* was translated into thirteen languages. Ferdinand Goetel's *From Day to Day* had affinities with the writing of James Joyce, and Witold Gombrowicz's *Ferdydurke* (1938) was a predecessor of the French anti-novel.

Leon Schiller, one of the most talented dramatists between the world wars, created monumental theater with masses of actors on a revolving stage.

The Nazi occupation of Poland ended all cultural and literary life on the surface. Many outstanding writers fled the country and others went underground to write of persecution and survival in a hostile world. During the war, underground theaters were giving performances in private apartments, and the future Pope

John Paul II, then Karol Wojtyła, was performing in them.

Two writers stayed in Poland. Adolf Rudnicki, born in Żabno in 1912 and known as the "Jeremiah of the Warsaw ghetto," wrote *The Flight from Yasnaya Polyana* (1949) and *The Dead and the Living Sea* (1952). The poetry of Zbigniew Herbert, born in Lwów in 1924, was heralded in England as "original and impressive."

Between 1945 and 1949 Leon Schiller continued to create, and Poland mourned the loss of Stefan Jaracz, the famous actor and director who died as a result of prison camp mistreatment.

The exiles included Marek Hłasko, born in Warsaw in 1934 and controversial because of his violent language and themes. In 1958, he defected to the West, where he died in the late 1960s. His renowned short novel is *The Eighth Day of the Week* (1956).

Czesław Miłosz, winner of the 1980 Nobel Prize for literature, was a member of the Warsaw underground and clandestinely published an anthology of poems, *Independent Song*, in 1942. He entered diplomatic service in 1946 and was stationed in Washington and Paris. He broke with the Warsaw government in 1951, and after a few years in Paris, came to California, where he is a professor of Slavic languages at the University of California, Berkeley.

Tadeusz Różewicz, born in 1921, wrote Theater of the Absurd plays after 1956, and Stanisław Grochowiak, born in 1934, is a New Wave playwright.

Jerzy Kosinski, born in 1933 in Łódź, came to the United States in 1957. His novel *The Painted Bird*, about an abandoned child wandering through war-torn Europe, is considered to be among the best literature of World War II. He has won a Guggenheim fellowship, and he received the National Book Award in 1969. His other books include *Steps* and *Being There*.

Sławomir Mrożek wrote *Tango* (1964), judged by some to be the best play of the post-World War II period.

Isaac Bashevis Singer, born in Poland in 1904, writes in Yiddish about the Polish Jewish ghetto. He won the Nobel Prize for Literature in 1982.

While it doesn't qualify as Polish literature, James Michener's *Poland*, a novelistic treatment of the intricacies of Polish history, has found wide readership.

Music and the Visual Arts

The great contribution of Polish talent and traditions in music and the arts places Poland high on the list of contributors to the grand American blend of peoples and cultures.

Music has been a part of life in Poland for thousands of years. Whistles and instruments of bone, wood, and clay have been found in archaeological excavations or have been pictured in the earliest art works.

The earliest tunes were folk music, lullabies, and dance rhythms. The arrival of Christianity in the tenth century brought the Gregorian chant. Polish liturgical music dates from the thirteenth century, as does *Bogurodzica* (Mother of God), which was often sung by Polish knights on their way to battle.

In the sixteenth century the organ and the lute were popular, and *Melodie na Psałterz Polski* (Melodies for the Polish Psalter), a collection of 150 pieces with a tilt toward Polish patriotism, was published by Mikołaj Gomołka, who wrote "These are not for Italians, but for the Poles."

The Polish musicians were prolific. Oskar Kolberg (1814-1890) and others collected more than 200,000 songs and dances. This work survived destructive wars and was republished in the 1960s.

Recording of Polish music began in the early 1900s. By 1939 some twenty-five thousand recordings had been saved only to be destroyed in World War II. Since 1945, however, Marian Sobieski and his wife Jadwiga have collected about seventy-five thousand recordings that are in the Institute of Fine Arts at Warsaw.

Opera dates from 1602 in Italy, and by 1650 at least a dozen operas, some with ballet, had been performed for the king of Poland. Poland's first opera house was built in 1724. By 1745 Jacek Szczurowski had written the first Polish symphony, and in 1778 the first public opera in Polish (Maciej Kamieński's *Nędza uszczęśliwiona*) was performed.

Stanisław Moniuszko (1819-1872) composed the operas *Halka* (1848) and *Straszny Dwór* (The Haunted Manor, 1869). Karol

Lipinski (1790-1861) had a violin competition with Paganini in Warsaw, played first violin in the orchestra of the Dresden Opera, and was conductor of the orchestra at the Saxon Court.

The Warsaw Philharmonic Orchestra was founded in 1901 and had world-renowned conductors in Emil Młynarski and Grzegorz Fitelberg.

Many musical artists performed for audiences in both Poland and the United States. Among the immigrants was Edward Sobolewski, composer of the opera *Monega, Flower of the Forest*, and the organizer in 1861 of the first symphony orchestra in Milwaukee, Wisconsin. Henryk Wieniawski, violinist and composer, toured the United States in 1872. Józef Hofmann, a piano child prodigy, came to the United States in 1887 and played more than 50 concerts. He later became musical director of the Curtis Institute of Philadelphia. Another piano prodigy to arrive in this country late in the nineteenth century was Zygmunt Stojowski.

Leopold Stokowski (Antoni Stanisław Bolesławowicz, 1882-1977), the brilliant orchestra conductor who was of Polish and Irish descent, was born in London and arrived in the United States as the century turned. He earned world-wide fame as conductor of the Philadelphia Orchestra, the NBC Symphony Orchestra, and others. His films with the Philadelphia Orchestra included Walt Disney's *Fantasia* in 1940. He wrote the book *Music for All of Us.*

Artur Rubinstein was born in Łódź in 1889 and made his piano debut at the age of twelve. Paderewski's protege, he played at Carnegie Hall in 1937 to a cheering audience, and had a long and distinguished American artistic career.

Harpsichordist Wanda Landowska, a graduate of the Warsaw Conservatory of Music, made her American debut in 1923 and settled in the United States after World War II.

Artur Rodziński developed the Cleveland Orchestra, beginning in 1933, and in 1943 became conductor of the New York Philharmonic.

Michal Urbaniak, whose jazz group Fusion plays in New York's Greenwich Village, came to the United States from Poland in the 1960s. Adam Makowicz is a jazz pianist and composer.

Poland has contributed memorable actors, both dramatic and operatic, to the stages of the world: Helena Modrzejewska

(Modjeska), a Shakespearean actress popular in the United States at the turn of the century; Jan and Edouard de Reszke, who sang Wagnerian opera at the Metropolitan Opera in New York; and Marcella Sembrich-Kochańska, lyric and coloratura soprano at the Met until her retirement in 1909.

Jan Kiepura, the Warsaw Opera's celebrated tenor, joined the Metropolitan Opera Company in New York in 1938, and Elżbieta Szczygielska, born in 1950 to Polish refugee parents in Detroit, went to Warsaw for her operatic training. Other Metropolitan Opera stars include Wiesław Ochman, Teresa Zylis-Gara, and Teresa Kubiak.

Stanisław Skrowaczewski came to the United States in the 1950s as guest conductor of the Cleveland and Pittsburgh orchestras, and later became conductor of the Minneapolis Symphony Orchestra, founded a century earlier by Edward Sobolewski.

Poland has a long tradition in the visual and decorative arts. Early medieval art includes Wit Stwosz's altar in St. Mary's church in Kraków and the Gothic sculptures of the Gniezno Door, depicting the life of St. Adalbert.

The Renaissance blossomed in Poland, resulting in the great castles and palaces in Kraków and Zamość. Many foreign and Polish artists were active in Poland during the Renaissance and the baroque and rococo periods. Polish noblemen and the last Polish king, Stanisław August Poniatowski, were patrons of the arts.

The nineteenth century initially represented a romantic trend in art. The best known painters of this period are Piotr Michałowski and Aleksander Orłowski, who painted many scenes of horses. Artur Grottger and Jan Matejko became famous for their historic paintings. In the final years of the century, the most famous artists were those who studied in Munich: Józef Chełmonski and Alfred Wierusz Kowalski and Aleksander and Maksymilian Gierymski, known for scenes of everyday life.

Modern Polish art includes world-renowned artists: Tadeusz Kantor, famous for his Cricot theatre and serious compositions; Magdalena Abakanowicz, tapestry; and Jozef Szajna, three-dimensional compositions and theatrical performances. The first avant-garde Polish artist to act in Chicago was the late Stanisław Szukalski, who died in 1988 in Los Angeles.

81

In large American cities there are colonies of young Polish artists. Illustrations by Andrzej Czeczot appear in *The New York Times*, *The New Yorker*, and *Atlantic Monthly*. Maciek Albrecht, Rafał Olbinski, and Bartek Małysa are often represented in American periodicals and exhibit in New York, where one can also see works by Zbigniew Krygier, Wojciech Fangor and others. In Chicago, Mirosław Rogala is one of the recognized video and computer graphic artists at the Art Institute of Chicago.

Yan Khur (Jan Kuracinski) has been recognized for his contemporary "biological structures to express human commitments and problems," called Ero-Art. Richard Anuszkiewicz is a Polish-American creator of Op Art.

In America there are many collectors of Polish art. Major exhibitions of Polish art include a 1989 touring exhibition of nineteenth-century Polish paintings shown in New York City, Washington, D.C., and Chicago.

Monumental art in the United States includes Jan Styka's *Golgotha* at Forest Lawn Memorial Park in Glendale, California. The painting was first shown in Warsaw in 1895 and then sent to America in a ship filled with immigrants. No building large enough to house the 195-by-45-foot canvas could be found. It was rolled up in storage for more than a generation until Dr. Hubert Eaton built the Hall of the Crucifixion in Forest Lawn to accommodate it.

Detail of Jan Styka's painting of the crucifixion exhibited at Forest Lawn

World's Largest Sculpture

Sculptor Korczak and Ruth Ziolkowski married in 1960 and worked in partnership on the Crazy Horse Memorial until his death in 1982.

Creating the world's largest sculpture was the life's work of Korczak Ziolkowski, a Polish American born September 6, 1908, in Boston. Korczak, as he liked to be called, designed the Crazy Horse Memorial being carved out of Thunderhead Mountain in South Dakota and worked on it for thirty-four years. After his death in 1982, his wife and family have continued the work, which will likely take decades more to complete.

The finished sculpture, at 563 feet high, will be eight feet taller than the Washington Monument, almost twice as tall as the Statue of Liberty and longer than two football fields. The four heads of Mount Rushmore, seventeen miles away, could fit inside the head of Crazy Horse, with room to spare.

Korczak, an orphan, learned the construction trades from a foster father and demonstrated his artistic skill as a teen-ager. At eighteen, he hand-crafted a grandfather's clock from fifty-five pieces of Santo Domingo mahogany.

In 1932, he used a coal chisel to carve his first portrait, a marble tribute to Frederick Pickering Cabot, the Boston juvenile judge who befriended Korczak and introduced him to the fine arts. Korczak was a studio sculptor and member of the National Sculpture Society in 1939, when his marble portrait, "Paderewski: Study of an Immortal," won first prize for sculpture by popular vote at the New York World's Fair.

That summer Korczak worked briefly for the sculptor who created Mount Rushmore. Sioux Indian chiefs asked Korczak to create a memorial to Crazy Horse, who led the victorious Indians in the Battle of the Little Bighorn. Chief Henry Standing Bear wrote to Korczak: "My fellow chiefs and I would like the white man to know the red man has great heroes, too."

Korczak pondered the proposal for seven years. He visited the Pine Ridge Indian Reservation in 1940, then returned to New England and spent two years sculpting a statue of Noah Webster as a gift to West Hartford, Connecticut. He was a volunteer in the United States Army during World War II, landed on Omaha Beach and later was wounded. After the war, he turned down the government's offer to create war memorials in Europe and accepted the Indians' invitation to create the Crazy Horse Memorial.

Korczak, then thirty-eight, came to South Dakota May 3, 1947, and lived in a tent while building a log studio-home, roads, and utilities. June 3, 1948, the memorial was dedicated and Korczak made his first blast on the mountain. Special guests included five of the nine living survivors of the Battle of the Little Big Horn.

Korczak's belief in the free enterprise system and his disapproval of the government's treatment of the Indians made him determined to keep Crazy Horse a non-profit educational and cultural humanitarian project. He would twice turn down $10 million in potential government aid. The government shouldn't be involved, he said, because it broke treaties with the Indians. Admission fees, sales of Native American arts and souvenirs, and donations of money, equipment and services finance the project.

In 1949, Korczak worked alone, blasting 97,000 tons off the mountain and running a small gas-powered jackhammer at the bottom of the mountain. The next year he married Ruth Ross, a student volunteer for the Noah Webster sculpture. Eighteen years younger than her husband, she became a partner in the Crazy Horse project, in which their ten children also would be involved.

In 1951, Korczak painted an outline of Crazy Horse on the mountain. It took 176 gallons of paint. A couple of years later, Korczak bought his first bulldozer. Summers, Korcazk and his family worked on the sculpture. In the winter, they added buildings to the visitors' center and their home. They also operated a dairy farm and lumber mill Korczak established.

Korczak with Lakota Chief Henry Standing Bear at the dedication June 3, 1948, of the Crazy Horse Memorial.

Work on the mountain was slow and painstaking. By 1968, Korczak was ready to begin tunneling through the mountain for what would be the opening under Crazy Horse's arm. It took two years of tunneling just to reach daylight.

The heavy work took its toll. Before his death, Korczak would have four back surgeries to remove six discs. He battled diabetes and arthritis and had two heart attacks and a quadruple bypass.

As Korczak lay dying October 20, 1982, his parting words to his wife were : "You must work on the mountain—but go slowly so you do it right." He is buried in the tomb he and his sons blasted into rock near the mountain. He wrote his own epitaph: "Korczak —Storyteller in Stone. May His Remains Be Unknown."

Ruth now supervises the mountain project, with the assistance of seven of the Ziolkowski sons and daughters and now grandchildren. Crazy Horse's face is scheduled for completion by 1998. The goal is to dedicate the nine-story face June 3, 1998, the 50th anniversary of the dedication of the memorial.

More than one million visitors a year watch the progress and visit the continually expanding Indian Museum of North America as well as Korczak's log-house studio, the first building at Crazy Horse. His work on display includes a Polish eagle made from the same marble used to carve the Noah Webster statue.

Construction of a Native American Educational and Cultural Center began in 1995. Future plans for the site include the University and Medical Training Center for the North American Indian.

Although Crazy Horse consumed most of Korczak's time, he continued to do other sculptures through the years. His memorial of Sitting Bull, carved from Crazy Horse granite, weighed almost seven tons. His gift to the city of Deadwood, South Dakota, was a 3,000-pound statue of Wild Bill Hickok. He gave his mahogany portrait of Chief Standing Bear to President John F. Kennedy. In 1983, Pope John Paul II accepted a bronze of the Crazy Horse scale model mounted on granite from the mountain. A similar model and a bronze sculpture of John F. Kennedy were presented to President Bill Clinton at the White House in 1993.

Korczak's mahogany *Fighting Stallions* was a favorite of South Dakota Governor George S. Mickelson, who was seven when he helped his father, Governor George T. Mickelson, set off the first blast for the Crazy Horse Memorial. After the younger Mickelson and seven others died in an airplane crash in 1993, the legislature chose as a memorial on the capitol lawn a larger-than-life bronze of *Fighting Stallions*. Ruth Ziolkowski donated the casting rights.

Korczak's many honors include tributes from the American Polish Engineering Association in 1984, the American Council for Polish Culture in 1990, and the American Institute of Polish Culture in 1993. May 3 is Korczak Day in South Dakota, and Korczak and Ruth are in the South Dakota Hall of Fame.

The Crazy Horse Memorial, the 563-foot-high mountain carving seen from about a mile away, eventually will look like sculptor Korczak Ziolkowski's scale model in the foreground. The scale model is at the Indian Museum of North America.

By May 1995, the nine-story-high face of Crazy Horse was taking shape. The eyes and nose had been substantially completed, and work on the Indian's lips had begun. The face is scheduled for completion by June 2, 1998, but finishing the entire mountain carving will take more decades.

Crazy Horse Memorial photos by Robb DeWall

87

Polish Customs

Warm Memories of the Past

The most enduring Polish customs are entwined with traditions of the church, and the Christmas season is particularly rich in time-honored practices. In the old days, Advent began on St. Martin's Day, November 12. On this day a goose would be roasted and the force of winter could be foretold by the color of its bones.

The vigil of St. Andrew's day, November 30, gave a young girl the opportunity to foresee her future. At midnight she would pour melted wax on water through a golden ring tied to a hair from her head or through a large keyhole, symbolic of the key to the future. She would carefully lift the resulting shape and interpret its shadow on the wall. Perhaps she would see the figure of a man, her bridegroom-to-be, or the tool of her future husband's trade, or a bridal wreath. This custom is popular in Poland today. Later, the Advent season was shortened, beginning shortly before December 6, when St. Nicholas arrives to reward good children. Misbehaving children might get gilded sticks. In Poland St. Nicholas asks catechism questions.

Wafers called *opłatki* are distributed at church for Christmas Eve supper, *wigilia*. The wafer is shared as the first food of the Christmas vigil. Sometimes at supper the wafer is touched with honey. In a beautiful tradition, when the wafer is broken and shared, it is also touched with the power of mutual forgiveness for any and all slights or differences of the past year. The wafer often produces scenes of reconciliation. Often the wafers are enclosed with Christmas cards for sharing across the miles. American Polish congregations share the wafer following midnight Mass at their churches.

In the country, a piece of wafer or a whole wafer might be placed under each plate. Following the meal, if the wafer stuck to the plate, it was a sign of a bountiful harvest. Rev. Czesław M. Krysa recalls being told that when his godmother's husband was a child, he would moisten the bottom of his plate to assure the sticking of the wafer.

Hay is placed under the tablecloth. Hay is symbolic of the manger where Christ was born. The tablecloth is white, symbolizing Mary's veil. Sheaves of the four principal grains—wheat, rye, oats, and barley—are placed in each corner of the room. Supper begins when the first star is sighted. The celebration includes singing *kolędy*, Polish Christmas carols. The uneaten food is left on the table for anyone who might come in. In times past, this was a way of sharing with the dear departed. Following the meal, blades of straw are pulled from beneath the tablecloth. The longer the blade, the longer one will live. Pastel-colored *opłatki* wafers are given to domestic animals and sometimes to pets. Sharing with the animals was a part of the first Christmas.

The Christmas Eve dinner traditionally has an odd number of courses, and thirteen courses are common, for Christ and the twelve apostles. Traditional dishes include herring or pike or carp, mushroom soup, sauerkraut, *pierogi* (dumplings), noodles with poppyseed and honey, fruit compote, and poppy-seed rolls with honey liqueur.

The *Pasterka* (Shepherd's Mass) is at midnight. According to a time-honored Polish tradition, midnight, the hour of Christ's birth, so transformed creation that the earth opened to show its treasures, the water in wells turned to wine, stones moved, each blade of grass rejoiced, and the animals conversed in human speech which only the pure in heart could hear.

In the eighteenth century Polish churches abandoned the custom of Christmas performances of the nativity with puppets. This gave rise to a door-to-door custom. In an especially beautiful tradition, the *gwiazdorzy* (star carriers) come caroling, bearing homemade lighted stars on poles and nativity scene creches.

According to an old custom, if you keep track of the weather during the twelve days of Christmas, you will have an indication of weather during the next twelve months.

Some Poles save scales from the Christmas dinner fish and carry them in their purses as a reminder "to keep the purse full of money in the coming year." On the last day of the year, as Poles visit each other, they give small change as good luck reminders to keep money available all year. They spread it from the entrance throughout the home. Before the New Year, on the feast of St. Stephen, all

The folk customs of Poland are depicted in this drawing by Alice Wadowski-Bak of the Christmas Eve supper (wigilia). The father breaks the wafer as the first star appears in the sky. Hanging over the table is the pająk (spider of straw), a chandelier-type ornament made of colored paper and straw. A small szopka (crèche scene) sits on the painted chest. Over the chest are Easter palms decorating a glass painting of a saint. The crucifix hangs on the highest point on the wall. Garlands hung from the four corners of the room symbolize the four corners of the world. A sheaf of wheat in the corner will later be spread on the fields and in the orchards for good luck in the coming year. The empty chair is for Christ or an unexpected guest, or in memory of a departed family member.

old business accounts must be settled.

New Year's Day is St. Sylvester's Day, commemorating the hero who in 317 imprisoned the dragon Leviathan for a thousand years. Expecting the beast to break loose in 1317, some were greatly relieved that it did not happen. New Year's Day is often celebrated with fireworks and political speeches.

On Epiphany, the Feast of the Magi, chalk, incense, and myrrh are blessed in church, and chalk is used over the main entrance of doorways to write the initials of the three kings, separated by crosses, thus: 19 † K † M † B † 96 with each year advancing by one over the previous year. The sign remains until the end of the year. In Poland a priest writes the letters on the doors as he visits the homes of parishioners and pronounces the Christmas blessing.

At Candlemas, February 2, honoring the Presentation of Our

Lord in the Temple, Poles observe *Matka Boska Gromniczna*. Candles blessed in church are taken home as a symbol of the Blessed Mother. They are called thunder candles. The candle is lit during thunderstorms to protect the home from lightning. It is also lit during times of trouble or when someone is approaching death. The legend surrounding the candles is that in the evening the Blessed Mother wards off wolves by using the candle as a torch. In the art gallery of the Orchard Lake Schools in Michigan, there is a painting of the Blessed Mother with the candle, warding off wolves. At the Carmelite Shrines in Munster, Indiana, there is a marble relief sculpture of the same theme.

The season of gaiety is *Karnawał*, the period between Christmas and Lent. That is the time for sleigh parties called *kulig*.

Tłusty Czwartek (Fat Thursday) before Ash Wednesday is the time to eat jelly doughnuts, *pączki* (pronounced "punch-key"). This joyous activity precedes the *Gorzkie Żale* (lamentation services) of Lent in Poland. Long lines form in front of all the bakeries in Poland, and millions of the jelly doughnuts are sold.

In America, jelly doughnuts are traditional for *Pączki* Day, the Tuesday before Ash Wednesday. Polka bands entertain on *Pączki* Day at the Polish-American bakeries of Hamtramck, Michigan. In Detroit, supermarket chains and doughnut shops carry *pączki* the week before Lent.

Churches in Poland use pussy willow branches instead of palms to be blessed on Palm Sunday. In an earlier day, hitting the legs of small children with pussy willow switches—to make them "good" and "pure" in the coming year—was practiced on Palm Sunday or Good Friday, and children were encouraged to swallow the catkins to ward off sore throats.

A sepulcher is built in every church, and sometimes the especially devout keep an all-night vigil before it. Every church in Poland is decorated with a scene of the grave of Christ. In certain cities there is a competition between churches for the most beautiful sepulcher. The people visit the sepulchers in various churches. This custom also prevails in Buffalo, New York.

In Polonia and in Poland, the food of the Easter breakfast is carried to the church and blessed on Holy Saturday. *Święconka* is the word for the blessed Easter foods and the meal at which they are

Eggs, sausage, a butter lamb, and bread with cross are the contents of a święconka *basket taken to a priest for blessing on Easter morning.*

eaten. Water blessed at the vigil on Holy Saturday is taken home.

In the basket, Easter foods to be blessed may include a small lamb carved from butter or marzipan; a round loaf of bread with a cross; a special yeast bread, *babka;* Polish sausage *(kiełbasa);* and the eggs of Easter. Horseradish, salt, and pepper may be included to symbolize all spices. In Poland a piece of sausage or ham, a piece of bread, salt, and a hard-boiled egg are taken for blessing.

The *święconka* breakfast includes foods with symbolic meanings. Christ is represented by a butter lamb carrying a banner of victory. The top of the Easter bread loaf or roll is marked with a cross. The eggs, preferably dyed, are a symbol of Christ's tomb and the resurrection. Often family members share a blessed egg with horseradish and salt at the beginning of the Easter meal. And of course there is Polish sausage (*kiełbasa*).

Drawing by Diane Heusinkveld

Pisanki, *the colorful eggs of Easter, are a symbol of Christ's tomb and the resurrection.*

Polish Americans continue to serve Easter foods according to tradition. In downtown Buffalo, New York, 100,000 people, mostly Poles, visit the historic Broadway Market to buy Easter foods. That is about ten times the usual traffic.

With Polish-American Catholics moving to the suburbs and joining Catholic parishes that contain other ethnic groups, there is discussion of which Polish traditions to keep. In Dearborn Heights, Michigan, Shirley Ann Galanty says the non-Polish people in her church liked the tradition of blessing the Easter baskets and have asked that the custom be kept. In Winona, Minnesota, St. Stanislaus parish retains the blessing of the Easter baskets, but because of a dwindling Polish-American membership does not have the breaking of the *opłatki* wafers after midnight Mass at Christmas.

An exhibition at the Buscaglia-Castellani Art Gallery at Niagara University at Niagara Falls, New York, featured photographs of Polish Easter baskets and their coverings, taken by Marion Faller, and a catalog of the exhibition by the guest curator, Kate Koperski.

In the 1920s, immigrant women caring for large families and sometimes boarders did not embroider the cloths but instead crocheted basket covers. In recent years, today's busy woman may cover the baskets with foil. Within the basket, there is a great deal of variation in contents and arrangements.

Dyngus Day, Easter Monday, is filled with frivolity. Boys sprinkle or douse girls with water. The girl who changes her clothes most frequently wins the popularity contest. In America, *Dyngus* Day is celebrated with polka bands and feasting. Radio stations and bars in Buffalo, New York; South Bend, Indiana; and elsewhere celebrate *Dyngus* Day. At Notre Dame University in South Bend, students and others have been known to celebrate a second *Dyngus* Day in the hot midsummer when things get dull.

Old agricultural customs in the Slavic world included the drowning of winter, greeting of spring, and the blessing of seeds. The celebration, with roots in pre-Christian times, is called *topienie marzanny*. Human-sized straw dolls are drowned.

At Pentecost *(Zielone Świątki)*, houses, doors, roadside shrines, and churches in Poland are decorated with tree branches. This custom has been merged with the Feast of Corpus Christi and its four outdoor altars. The faithful go to the outdoor altars prepared at various homes. Several parishes in the Buffalo and Toledo areas celebrate this public manifestation of religious fervor.

Zielone Świątki means "green holidays" and is celebrated when the leaves are out. At Lwów, a former city of Poland, now in Ukraine, the former Communist government closed all Catholic churches except the cathedral, but often green wreaths "sprouted" on the doors of closed churches as a sign that the Holy Spirit (green) was still alive.

Wianki (wreath floating) on St. John's Eve (Midsummmer's Eve) is an old custom now practiced in the United States as a picturesque ceremony. In Washington, D.C., wreaths are floated in the reflecting pool of the Washington Monument. At Orchard Lake Schools, Orchard Lake, Michigan, bonfires light the grounds and wreaths with candles are floated on the lake.

In Poland's peasant culture the wreath is a symbol of virginity. On St. John's Eve girls make special wreaths with herbs, flowers, and candles. If the wreath floats, legend says the girl will marry that year. Young men wait at the side of the water to catch the wreaths. Elaborate water floats, folk dancing, light shows, and fireworks are an annual event in Kraków at the Wawel Castle on the Vistula River.

On the Feast of the Assumption, August 15, bouquets of field flowers, herbs, and grains are brought to *Matka Boska Zielna*, Our Lady of the Herbs, to be blessed. A ceremony called *Dożynki* celebrates the end of the harvest. Wreaths made of the current year's harvest plants are blessed in the church and kept for a year.

After the ceremony of a Polish wedding, the bride's mother greets the couple with bread and salt. The bride kisses the bread. Bread is the staple, the staff of life symbolic of all food. Salt is that which preserves. Anyone who comes to a home for the first time is greeted with bread and salt. The wedding couple is greeted as a new person.

Historically, altar candles at wedding ceremonies are watched carefully. If one goes out, it is said to presage the early death of the partner on that side of the altar. A rainy wedding day is considered to be unlucky, but the bride's tears are a good omen.

An early Polish-American custom at wedding parties was to break a heavy dinner plate by hitting it with a silver dollar. The coin could not be retrieved for a second try, but some paid to break a plate with their feet.

In Buffalo, New York, a song about the twelve angels is sung with each of the angels bringing a gift for the bride. An angel brings a fragrant lily, a burning candle, and a ring symbolic of married life. The song is sung to the *oberek* dance rhythm that is more Polish than the polka. A record shop in Buffalo provides English and Polish song sheets to couples for their wedding receptions. The maid of honor and other married women do the *oczepiny*, a ritual symbolizing the transition from maiden to wife. The bride's veil is removed and replaced with a housemaid's cap while the women sing of the pains and pleasures of married life. In some circles wedding guests pay to dance with the bride, dropping coins or dollar bills into an apron held by one of the attendants. This is "bride's money" to be spent only as she wishes. At the end, a hymn "Beloved Mother" is sung to the Blessed Mother. The next day all the leftover foods might be served at a second wedding reception called the *poprawiny*, a word meaning "to make it better."

For a baby's baptism, the godfather and godmother traditionally carry the baby to the church. Less joyous is the *stypa*, the reception after a funeral. This is a part of Polish mourning. The most widely practiced Polish customs in America are the Christmas *wigilia*, the Easter *święconka*, and the *stypa* after the funeral.

Above: Traditional Polish costumes, including the bridal gown at right, are featured in the Polish Museum of America in Chicago, Illinois.

At left: Jolanta Mazewski-Dryden is director of the Polish Eagle Dancers of Houston, Texas.

1988 photograph

The market in Buffalo, New York, is especially busy at Easter.

Traditional Folk Arts

Poland has one of Europe's richest folk art traditions. Fed by religious events and themes, Polish creativity took the form of woodcarving, paper cutting *(wycinanki)*, weaving and textile design, egg decorating, wreath-making with flowers and grasses, painting on glass, and embroidery.

The drab realities of peasant life were relieved by richly decorated festival clothing and brightly colored chests to hold the family linens.

In the homes of more prosperous peasants, the *biały pokój* (white room) showcased the fine needlework of the household's women. A bed might be covered with a linen spread magnificently embroidered and inset with bands of lace. The embroidered cases on plump down pillows, also adorned with embroidery and lace, would be interwoven with bright ribbons to draw the coverings taut.

Lace was created by bobbin, crochet, and knitting techniques. In the nineteenth century, embroidery on tulle or fine net became popular, and net bonnets were worn in almost every region of Poland.

Woodcarving began with farmers in remote villages who spent the long, snowbound winters creating figures with pocket knives. Because religion was uppermost in their thinking, they frequently replicated the statues in their churches and shrines. Some carvers added variations that reflected their own lives, such as large and gnarled hands that spoke of hard labor, and faces with sad and worried expressions that bespoke their own outlook.

According to Rev. Czesław M. Krysa of the Orchard Lake Schools, Orchard Lake, Michigan, Polish tradition held that the threshold of a home and intersections of streets were crossroads, points of tension. Therefore, a cross or a holy image was placed above the doorway, and holy figures were enshrined where streets met and crossed.

Roadside shrines were placed at the sites of accidents to make restitution, or purify the spots. Many of these contained the typical Polish "worrying Christ" who resembled a Polish peasant, crowned with thorns and carved of wood.

Sometimes entire families of carvers formed dynasties that extended into several generations, and some villages were known for their numerous and excellent carvers.

Other folk sculptures are in salt and coal mines. The salt mine at Wieliczka has centuries-old underground chapels and salt sculptures, mostly of religious subjects. The most famous is the Saint Kinga Chapel. Saint Kinga is a patron of miners. Coal sculptures are in the coal mines of Silesia.

A decline of Polish folk sculpture began during World War I and continued during World War II. Furthermore, industrialization wiped out the village settings where the tradition was nourished. A government cooperative known as *Cepelia*, however, now promotes the works of folk artists and sells them in Poland and abroad. A certain stylization and sophistication has resulted, but collectors still can find the primitive pieces that made the art form so endearing.

Larch is the preferred wood for carving because it is easily worked and is available throughout Poland. Even so, many carvers choose oak, cherry, or apple wood. The pocket knife is still the tool of preference. Some of the folk artists color their figures and others leave them in the natural wood.

Creators of many of the older carvings are unknown. They feared public ridicule and did not acknowledge their own work. If they were alive today, they would be pleased to know that fine art museums now exhibit their work.

Paper cutting as an art *(wycinanki)* became popular in Poland in the nineteenth century, when paper became readily available. Designs were cut to decorate the home. At Christmas and at Easter, when the house was cleaned and whitewashed, new *wycinanki* were created. Exposed ceiling beams supported long, horizontal designs. Large, complex cutouts depicting daily life and celebrations adorned the doors.

Egg decorating *(pisanki)*, "writing" designs in wax before dyeing the egg, is an ancient practice in Poland, where they tell the legend of Mary Magdalene carrying eggs to the tomb of Jesus. When she told the apostles that Christ had risen, they said, "Lady, do not bother us." She showed them the eggs, which changed into brilliantly colored *pisanki* before their eyes. Still skeptical, the apostles were finally convinced when nightingales hatched from the *pisanki* singing "Alleluia!"

Archaeologists excavating in Opole in the mid-1950s found decorated eggshells and one intact egg dating from the tenth century. The designs were similar to those of contemporary *pisanki*.

The eggshell symbolizes the tomb, and its yolk prefigures the sun of Easter morn rising out of the tomb. Originally, all eggs were dyed brick red. The color was derived from onion skins and was symbolic of Christ's redeeming blood. Traditional designs include stylized flowers, ladders, hearts, triangles, stars, fir trees, grapevines, wavy lines for water, pussy willows, the sun, snails, and birds.

Kraszanki are eggs dyed a single color with no design. Natural dyes are made from onion skins, beets, young rye shoots, and birch bark. The eggs are taken to a priest to be blessed, and are eaten by Polish and Polish-American families on Easter morning.

In several regions of Poland *nalepianki* (paper eggs) are created by gluing bright scraps of paper, straw, or bits of fabric to hollow eggs. The eggs sometimes are incorporated in *pająki* (mobiles) hung from a circular frame.

Before the Christmas tree came to Poland, one way of decorating a cottage was to suspend from the ceiling a large spiderweb mobile *(pająk)* created from straw, eggs, crepe paper, or whatever might be found in the house. Legend has it that the Virgin Mary had no clothes for her baby, and the spider wove a silken cloth for the Savior's first garment. Later the smaller *pająki* were made to hang on the Christmas tree. Polish Christmas ornaments are also made from hollow eggshells transformed into birds, fish and hatted heads with colored paper, fabric, and glue.

Polish Americans are experiencing a new surge of interest in the folk arts of their ancestral country, and classes in egg decorating and paper cutting are offered occasionally in the larger communities, as well as on the campus of the Orchard Lake Schools. The color and beauty of the nation's folk art has enhanced the sense of Polish identity through the centuries, and now Polish Americans are collecting such art for that same sense of identity.

How to 'Write a Polish Easter Egg

Pisanki—egg decorating—comes from the Polish word pisać, *meaning "to write."*

By Rev. Czesław M. Krysa

Supplies: Medium-sized, raw eggs at room temperature, vinegar, small cake of beeswax, candle (taper) in a low stand, *pisak* or stylus, aniline dyes (yellow, orange, green, red, violet, brown, black) prepared in water and vinegar, spoon, paper towels, tissues, one large and one small safety pin, stiff wire (6" long), small bowl, clear glossy varnish, waxed paper.

Step by Step

1. Wipe the egg with a paper towel moistened in some vinegar. Heat the metal ends of the stylus over the candle flame. The hot stylus is touched to the beeswax to form a puddle of molten wax which enters the stylus and becomes the "ink" in this batik process.

2. Write with the molten wax on the egg. Always write away from yourself, turning the egg when necessary. The dye will not color the molten wax; hence, a batik process. The egg is divided into eight sections. From each intersecting point write a small curled cane, always working away from yourself and turning the egg when necessary.

3. Place in the yellow dye bath.

4. Remove from the yellow dye bath after about 10 minutes and pat dry with a paper towel. Allow the egg to set for 5 minutes.

5. Write the rungs of the ladders on the yellow egg. After completing the rungs, place the egg into an orange dye, remove, and write the "teeth" on each final rung. Place into purple dye for about 10 minutes. Remove and let set until dry.

6. Hold the egg with the waxed portion next to candle flame (not over or in the candle flame to avoid scorching). When wax melts and turns shiny, quickly yet gently wipe off the molten wax with a facial tissue in one stroke. Repeat until the entire egg is cleaned.

7. To preserve the egg and deepen the colors, varnish using an index finger (two coats). Leave the egg to dry on waxed paper.

8. After the second coat has dried overnight, the contents are blown out by making a hole with the point of a small safety pin at one end large enough to insert a thin yet rigid wire. Break the yolk with the wire and gently scramble the contents. Make a small hole in the opposite end.

9. Gently, yet firmly clasp the egg and blow into the smaller hole; the scrambled contents will slowly be forced out through the larger hole.

Step 2

Step 3

Step 7

Step 6

Step 9

Frances Drwal of Posen, Illinois, collector and teacher of Polish folk art, holds a wycinanki *Christmas angel paper mobile. She collects paper cuts and crafts from Poland.*

Wycinanki—Papercuts

Cutting paper for decoration began in the rural homes of Poland. The people had to use the tools and supplies at hand. Sheep shears were available and were used to cut the paper. Traditionally, white and colored papers have been used. Polish cottages were decorated with *wycinanki*, many just before Easter after the walls were whitewashed. The craft was popular in the early twentieth century.

The paper may be folded once over or many times to make the cuts for ornamental work. Usually the cuts are in diagonal lines, according to Frances Drwal of Posen, Illinois. More complicated *wycinanki* are made by pasting layers of colored paper on top of each other.

Today the main regions where *wycinanki* are popular in Poland are Kurpie and Łowicz, where women and girls make the papercuts for people from the cities. Typical of the Kurpie region are one-color symmetrical papercuts showing forest or woodland scenes, those with symmetrical patterns in circles, and multi-colored ones showing roosters. Łowicz *wycinanki* are usually multicolored with stars, ribbons, or stripes often pasted onto eggshells.

Directions from Frances Drwal for making a *wycinanki* Christmas tree angel:

Equipment needed

Scissors
Colored felt tip markers
Black felt tip pen to outline
Paper

Glue (Elmer's)
Thin green thread
Fixative spray if desired

To make the angel shown on page 105:

1. Copy the angel pattern four times on a piece of paper, twice on each side back to back.

2. Color the angels using bright colors. Color each of the sides exactly the same way. Suggested colors: Wings—Color each section a different color. For example, yellow, orange, red, blue,

purple, green. Even the skirt can be colored this way. If you go over the dark lines heavily, the results will look like stained glass.

3. Cut out the angels. Fold each angel on dotted line.

4. With black felt-tip pen, go over all the cut lines and outline the entire design on both sides of each section. This outlining is not absolutely necessary, but it brings out the design and enhances the ornament.

5. Measure a piece of thread, preferably green. If you do not have green, color the thread green with the marker. Fold the thread in half, leaving a loop at the top for hanging.

6. Put a thin line of glue on the dotted line of one section of the design, down the middle, and place the thread on this line with the loop at the top for hanging. You may prefer putting the glue on the thread and then placing the thread on the bottom line of this section. After this dries in a few seconds, put a thin line of glue on the dotted line of the other section of the ornament. Place the folded edge of this part on the first section, dotted line to dotted line. Hold a minute, bonding the two sections together with the thread in the middle, loop sticking out on top. If a thread is hanging out at the bottom of the ornament, snip it.

Open up. Spray all sides with fixative. The more times you spray it, the more sturdy the ornament becomes, and it gives an almost transparent shine like stained glass. This also enhances and pre-serves the colors. Allow the ornament to dry a few minutes be-tween sprayings. You now have an eight-sided mobile ornament for your Christmas tree.

Angel pattern for a wycinanki *mobile by Frances Drwal*

A Visit to Poland

Far, far
Across the sea, far away
Is a beautiful land,
The native land of my mother. . .

So go the words of a song presented by a group from Sydney, Australia, at a festival in Poland of folklore groups from all over the world. Whether you are of Polish descent or not, a visit to Poland is a rewarding experience, especially since the Poles have thrown off the yoke of communism and are free.

The transition period has been difficult for citizens of Poland. Dramatic changes have taken place in government, in appearance, in attitudes. Polish cities and the countryside blossom with bright colors. Food is plentiful. There is new building everywhere. New businesses sprout up daily, but so do prices. The changes have caused much "out with the old and in with the new," but the changes cannot be implemented overnight. Unemployment has perhaps been the most difficult change for the average Pole. Rising prices, unbelievable inflation, and political problems are discouraging. The Poles, as do the Romans, have a saying: "Kraków was not built in a day." And slowly, things are looking up.

For tourists, the changes have also made a difference. Gone are the days of the black market. There are many new hotels and other places tourists can stay as well as new restaurants. Old palaces have been returned to original owners and restored as inns. The palaces are usually off the beaten path, but you are treated royally and the prices are often lower than at the hotels. It is no problem to rent a car and go on your own; many gas stations line the roads. Moneywise, Poland is still a bargain compared to western European countries.

Poland is about the size of the state of New Mexico. It has a variety of landscapes from the Baltic in the north to the Tatra Mountains, part of the Carpathians, in the south. Two weeks is appropriate for a first visit. A guided tour is suggested. Even if there are relatives to visit, it would be rare if they have the time or means to take visitors around the country. The Polish people are extremely hospitable, anxious to meet and talk with Americans, and many lasting friendships have begun this way.

Cultural offerings are many, and prices are low compared to the United States. You can attend the opera or theater and enjoy front row seats for ten dollars—if you go to the box office yourself. If you deal with an agency handling tickets in the hotels, you will pay twice as much. One group visiting Poland enjoyed a concert of contemporary music in Warsaw, the opera in Poznań, the American musical *My Fair Lady* in Kraków, and the old favorite *Merry Widow*, plus folklore shows with beautiful regional costumes.

Poles are well-educated and culturally, politically, and historically aware regarding not only Poland but other European countries and the United States. Don't be surprised if you are drawn into a political or philosophical discussion with Poles. Visitors have heard one gentleman, retired and a guide in a small museum in a mountain town, recite parts of the *Iliad* in Greek! He received a classical education, Latin and Greek included, at a high school in the mountain region.

It is a good idea to do some homework on Polish history and geography before your trip. It will make your trip much more meaningful. Videos on Polish cities and places to visit are available from the Polish National Tourist Bureau in Chicago or New York.

Suppose we begin our tour of Poland in its capital, Warsaw, which was almost totally destroyed by the Nazis during World War II. Most of its monuments and especially the Old Town, which includes the Royal Castle, have been rebuilt. Be sure to see the documentary film *But Still Warsaw* at the Warsaw Historical Museum in the Old Town. The film shows the tragic fate of the capital during World War II. Aside from the Royal Castle, St. John's Cathedral, the Market Place of the Old Town, and its charming burghers' houses, there is Łazienki Park with its palace and its beautiful and sad monument of Chopin under a willow tree. Here, on a Sunday afternoon, tourists may sit in the rose garden in the shadow of the monument and listen to piano concerts of Chopin's music. There is a beautiful architectural and park complex in which to view the Belvedere Palace and, further on, the Baroque

Palace in Wilanów and the Wilanów Poster Museum. Warsaw has forty-seven museums and thirty theaters! While in Warsaw, don't miss a side trip to Żelazowa Wola, Frederick Chopin's birthplace, which to this day resounds with his music. Not far from Warsaw are the folklore center of Łowicz and the town of Niepokalanów, where Saint Maximilian Kolbe, who was martyred in Auschwitz and was recently canonized by Pope John Paul II, had his mission center.

A thousand-year-old town on the Vistula River, which is the eternal symbol of Polishness, is Kraków, the capital of Poland for six centuries. The city itself is a museum with its Cloth Hall, Market Place, marvelous churches, and charming streets. It is a city in which to walk. Visit its National Museum which houses the most precious collections of Polish and foreign art, including Leonardo da Vinci's *Lady with an Ermine*. See the beautiful old buildings and courtyards of the Jagiellonian University, which was founded before Columbus discovered America and was attended by Nicholas Copernicus. Pause a moment at Wawel Hill to see the Royal Castle and Cathedral where Poland's kings were crowned, and where they lie buried with its poets and outstanding patriots and leaders. Thanks to the movie *Schindler's List*, filmed in Kraków, the Jewish quarter including the synagogue and cemetery has been almost fully restored.

A few kilometers from Kraków is Wieliczka, a town famous for its salt mine with awesome underground chambers, lakes, carvings and chapel (more like a cathedral with crystal salt chandeliers). This mine has been in use since the thirteenth century. Not far away is Oświęcim where in 1940 the Nazis set up a large concentration camp, Auschwitz. Here more than four million people of twenty-eight nationalities died. It is now a Museum of Martyrdom. And we must not forget Wadowice, the birthplace of Pope John Paul II, with its little museum where you can even see his skis!

The spiritual heart of Poland is Częstochowa, where the famous icon of the Black Madonna, *Matka Boska Częstochowska*, is housed. Here the Polish people have prayed to Our Lady for centuries. She is the Queen of Poland, and the faith of the people has never wavered. The ceremony of the unveiling of the Icon of Our Lady is unforgettable and every effort should be made to attend this heart-warming event.

Of course, you cannot miss Zakopane, Poland's winter resort in the Tatra Mountains. The *górale,* or highlanders, are a unique people with a rich folk culture. Their decorative costumes, the Zakopane style of architecture, the unique handicrafts—sculptures, glass paintings, wood carvings, and embroidery—must be seen to be fully appreciated. A great attraction of this region is a thrilling ride on rafts navigated by the highlanders down the Dunajec River gorge as you enjoy the towering scenery.

The city of Poznań is also worth a visit. Once the capital of Poland, it is now the city of the annual International Technological Poznań Fair. There you will find a tenth-century cathedral with the remains of the first Polish rulers. It is also a cultural center with a beautiful opera house and a town hall which is a treasury of art on the outside as well as inside. Not far from Poznań is a little jewel of a castle at Kórnik, complete with a castle ghost, the "Lady in White," who walks the halls at midnight! The castle is surrounded by a beautiful park with exotic plants and flowers. Gniezno, a capital of early Poland, is close by. It is the city associated with the rise and development of the Polish state. Its most priceless monument is its cathedral, begun in the tenth century, and renowned for its valuable art treasures and the bronze doors of St. Adalbert. Also in the Poznań vicinity is Biskupin, a unique wooden, ancient Slavic settlement of the fifth-sixth century B.C. And here you find an outdoor beehive museum—beehives built in shapes of a bear, a peasant woman, a Franciscan friar, buildings, and other items—unbelievable!

Poland's Baltic coast is the location of the tri-city of Gdańsk, Gdynia, and Sopot. Gdańsk, the former free city of Danzig, is a city to remember, the amber capital of Poland, its Royal Road along which you will see beautifully decorated houses, the Fountain of Neptune, the Golden Gate, and the largest church in Poland—the Gothic church of the Holy Virgin Mary. While in this vicinity, stop at Oliwa where at noon, in a thirteenth-century cathedral, you may attend a concert played on the largest and most beautiful organ in Poland. Also in the area is the peninsula of Westerplatte, where the first shots of World War II were fired; a monument honors the fallen defenders. Gdańsk is the birthplace of Solidarity. Its most famous citizen, Lech Wałęsa, was elected president of Poland in 1990. Gdynia is the ship-building port; tourists may visit the museum ship *Błyskawica* and the ocean-going sailing museum yacht *Dar Pomorza*, which was one of the tall ships in the 200th birthday celebration of the United States. Sopot is a seaside resort city on the Baltic. It has Europe's longest pier, called the *Molo*, on which you may stroll out into the Baltic. Here also the International Song Festival is held yearly in late August. Along the way from the tri-cities be sure to visit Malbork, the huge Gothic castle of the Order of Teutonic Knights, built in the thirteenth-fifteenth centuries, a magnificent example of medieval fortifications with powerful defense walls, towers, and gates.

These are some of the highlights of a visit to Poland. There are many more. In short, eastern Poland has the city of Lublin, as well as the Białowieża Forest, which contains the largest free-roaming herd of bison in the world. To the northeast, there are the beautiful forest lands and the Mazurian Lake District, often called "the land of ten thousand lakes."

You will not be able to see all of Poland in one short visit. Poland indeed has a lot for the tourist, and you will want to return again and again. To you who will embark on a journey to this beautiful and tragic land, we wish, as in the old Polish saying, *Szerokiej drogi!* (May the road you travel be wide) and may your pleasures be many.

—*Frances Drwal*

The Warsaw Royal Castle, destroyed by the Nazis during World War II, was restored in the 1970s and is now a public musem.

110

Polish Cooking

Ethnic cuisines depend mostly on availability of products. Poland has always been a country in which agriculture had a dominant position. Nearly all products grown in the moderate climate of Northern Europe can be found on Polish tables.

Pork is most popular for the everyday meal. For more elegant dining, the nod goes to game meat, such as hare, venison, or brawn, which is spiced or pickled boar or pig. Chicken is the everyday poultry selection, with duck or goose for Sunday dinner, and turkey for oc-

Jacek, holding daughter Anya, and Malgorzata Nowakowski.

casional dining. Fish for the table include trout, pike, pike-perch, bass, tench, catfish, flounder, and herring.

Boiled potatoes are a first-choice addition to meat, fish and poultry. Sometimes buckwheat, pilaf, or potato pancakes replace potatoes. Popular vegetables are celery root, cauliflower, tomato, bibb lettuce and, most popular of all, cabbage and string beans.

Typical beverages are tea, coffee (regular fine-ground coffee made like instant coffee), milk, sour milk (kefir, buttermilk), and fruit syrups diluted with water.

For breakfast, the Polish menu will consist of some kind of milk beverage (coffee with milk, cocoa with milk, tea with milk, or just hot milk), scrambled or soft-boiled eggs, rolls with butter, or cheese (farmer) or ham. Breakfast is usually eaten very early, depending on the work schedule.

The equivalent of American lunch is a light midday meal called second breakfast, eaten around noon. This usually consists of a light sandwich and a glass of tea or milk.

The main meal of the day is dinner, usually eaten around 4 p.m., again depending on the work schedule, and different on week-ends. A dinner is composed of two main dishes plus a salad and dessert. A bowl of soup or, on a hot summer day, a portion of pilaf, buckwheat, barley, or potatoes served with buttermilk or kefir makes the first dish. The second dish is composed of potatoes, buckwheat, or pilaf with meat, poultry, or fish. It can also be dumplings, blintzes (thin pancakes rolled with a filling of fruit or cottage cheese), or pancakes, served with no accompaniment. Boiled vegetables may be served in place of salad. Dessert is usually a piece of cake with a glass of tea or coffee.

The last meal of the day is a supper consisting of a small sandwich or some light dish such as pigs feet in aspic, meat cold-cuts, or fish in aspic.

For ordinary meals, Poles use utensils that are a little different. The cup, popular in America, is replaced by a glass of about the same capacity. Hearty soups are served in a bowl or a deep plate (as it is called in Poland). Thin soups may be served in a cup. Salads and cooked vegetables are served on individual plates or bowls. For elegant dining, table settings are quite like those of other European or American dinner tables.

The Polish way of cooking calls for all products to be "cooked to death" until they are really tender and soft. The meat—Polish style—has to melt in your mouth, and the same rule applies to all cooked vegetables.

Polish cuisine has a lot of influences inherited from the cuisines of ethnic minorities present in the former Polish territory, including Jewish, Ukrainian, Lithuanian, Russian, and German. Because Poland was "divided in three" during the entire nineteenth century and incorporated into Austro-Hungary, Prussia, and Russia, Polish cuisine adopted some of the favorites of those nations— breads and noodles from Austria, German meats, Russian borscht, Lithuanian boiled meatballs, et cetera.

Polish cuisine is generally tasty and nutritious. It is rich in breads, soups, dumplings, meat dishes, pancakes, and salads. So please enjoy your Polish food prepared from the recipes in this book and, most important, do not forget to say *Smacznego* to your table companions, as that is a matter of good manners in Poland. *Smacznego!*

—*Jacek Nowakowski*

Appetizers and Beverages

Polish Toast Song
A hundred years, may you live a hundred years!

Sto Lat
Sto lat, sto lat
Niech żyje, żyje nam
Jeszcze raz, jeszcze raz
Niech żyje nam!

This song is as popular as "For he's a jolly good fellow."

Mead
Miód Pitny

1 quart strained honey	pieces of ginger root
3 quarts water	nutmeg
1 teaspoon hops	piece of dried orange peel
1 teaspoon juniper berries	1 1/2 ounces fresh yeast

Cook the honey with the water for 1 hour. Take a piece of cheese-cloth and place the nutmeg, ginger, orange peel, hops, and juniper berries in it and tie it closed. Secure a weight on the end and place in the honey mixture. Boil another hour. Cool the honey and place in a carboy, an airtight container that will allow gases to escape, but will not allow air to enter. These can be found at wine and beer-making shops. Dissolve the yeast in a little of the honey mixture, then add to mead. Seal the carboy. Mead will ferment at room temperature for 6 months. When the mead is fermented the carboy will stop bubbling. Place the carboy in a cool dry place. After a year it will definitely be through fermenting and you can transfer the mead to bottles and seal the tops. Watch for delayed fermentation. If you see additional fermentation open the bottle to allow the fermentation to finish, then close again. If fermentation occurs in a sealed bottle, it will most likely blow up. The longer the mead sits the better it gets. Makes 1 gallon.

Spiced Vodka
Krupnik

Frances Drwal, Posen, Illinois

Frances is a teacher, lecturer, traveler, and folk artist. She says this is a famous drink.

1 1/2 cups honey
2/3 cup water
1 teaspoon vanilla or 1 vanilla
    bean
8 sticks cinnamon

3 whole cloves
1/4 teaspoon nutmeg
2 strips lemon peel, 2 inches
    each
1 bottle (1 liter) vodka

Mix the honey, water, vanilla, spices, and lemon peel in a large saucepan. Bring to a boil. Cover and simmer 5 minutes. Add the vodka and remove from heat. Serve hot or cold. Yields 1 quart.

Eggs in Mayonnaise
Jajka w Majonezie

4 hard-cooked eggs
1 1/2 cups mayonnaise
milk

lettuce, optional
tomato slices, optional

Peel and cut the eggs in half. Dilute the mayonnaise with a little milk. Place the eggs in a shallow serving dish and spread with mayonnaise. Decorate with the lettuce and tomatoes if desired. This is a great dish for small parties. Serves 4.

Eggs Stuffed with Mushrooms
Jaja Faszerowane z Pieczarkami

Henryka Woźniak
Warsaw, Poland

6 ounces mushrooms, chopped	1 teaspoon mayonnaise
1 teaspoon butter	salt and pepper to taste
5 hard-cooked eggs, with shell	chives or parsley, chopped
1 small bunch parsley, chopped	mayonnaise for garnish

Sauté the mushrooms in the butter, until soft. Carefully cut the eggs in half without peeling. Separate the egg yolks. Mash the egg yolks, add the chopped mushrooms, parsley, salt, and pepper. Blend together. Add the mayonnaise; mix. Place the mixture into the peeled egg whites, forming a mound on top. Arrange each egg half on a lettuce leaf. Garnish with a teaspoon of mayonnaise. Sprinkle with chives or parsley. Serves 5.

Easter Cheese

Feliksa Jelen
Philadelphia, Pennsylvania

3 pounds dry cottage cheese	3 ounces cream cheese
3 eggs	1/2 cup sour cream
2 teaspoons salt	

Mix all ingredients well. Put in a linen bag and tie the bag up to drip for a day. Place the bag between two boards and weight the boards with a large stone. Leave for 3 to 4 days. Remove the bag and keep it at room temperature to turn yellow for about 1/2 day. Refrigerate. Slice into chunks and enjoy. Makes about 3 1/2 pounds.

Pâté
Pasztet

2 tablespoons lard
1 pound lean beef
2 pounds pork
1 pound veal
1 pound hare or chicken
1 carrot, peeled
1 big parsley root
1 onion, quartered
1 1/2 pounds pork fat

10 peppercorns
1 bay leaf
1 pound pork liver
5-inch piece French bread
7 eggs
1/2 teaspoon nutmeg
salt to taste
1 teaspoon pepper

Melt the lard in a pan. Brown all the pieces of meat except liver, adding water to avoid burning. Add the carrot, parsley root, onion and pork fat. Add all the spices except nutmeg and pepper. Simmer, adding water until the meats are tender, about 2 to 3 hours. Add the liver and simmer for 10 more minutes, or until liver is cooked. Soak the French bread in meat sauce. In a blender grind the meat very finely in the following pattern: first beef, pork, half the bread, liver, veal, pork fat, hare, and the remaining bread. Blend everything together, adding the whole eggs, nutmeg, salt, and pepper. Knead the mixture like dough until smooth. Place the mixture in a greased and floured 7x11x2 1/2-inch pan. Bake at 400° for 20 minutes; reduce heat to 325° and bake for another 40 minutes. Serve cold as an appetizer or cold cut. Makes 8 pounds.

The Orchard Lake Schools art gallery houses 145 pieces of early and contemporary Polish folk sculpture collected by Barbara A. Michniowaka-Dietz of Long Island, New York.

Soups

Borscht
Barszcz

1/2 pound beef with bones
  or just beef bones
1 quart water
salt and pepper
3 pounds beets, peeled and
  sliced

juice of 1 lemon, divided
4 teaspoons sugar, divided
1 teaspoon flour
3/4 cup sour cream

Cook the beef and water to make a broth. Add the salt and pepper to taste. Set aside. Sprinkle the beets with salt and set aside for 3 hours. Cover beets with cold water and boil for 15 minutes. Add half of the lemon juice and a little sugar. Set aside for 1 hour. Skim off the beef broth and add to beets. In a separate pot, mix the flour with a little water and add to the borscht. Bring to a boil. Reduce heat. Add the sour cream, salt and the remaining sugar and lemon juice. Serve hot with boiled potatoes. Serves 4.

Beet Kvas

6 cups boiled water, cold
3 cooked beets, sliced

3 slices whole rye bread,
  crushed

Pour the water over the beets. Add the crushed whole rye bread. Let stand at room temperature for 3 to 5 days. Drain off the juice and use the clear liquid as a base for borscht. Makes 7 cups.

Lenten Borscht
Barszcz Wigilijny

One of the main dishes for the Christmas Eve dinner.

8 medium-sized beets, peeled
6 cups water
1 carrot, sliced
1 celery stalk, sliced
1 small parsley root, chopped
1 onion, sliced
1 leek, sliced
2 ounces dried mushrooms
a carp head, optional
1 teaspoon salt
salted dill*
1 garlic clove
1 pint beet kvas, recipe found
    on previous page
1 uncooked ground beet,
    optional
1 teaspoon butter
1 onion, sliced

In a quart of water boil the whole beets together with the sliced vegetables and mushrooms. Add the cleaned carp head, salt, whole salted dill and crushed garlic. When the beets are tender, take them out, strain and reserve the liquid; separate the mushrooms for dumplings. Slice the beets; add the beets and beet kvas to the liquid. To improve the color of the borscht add a ground fresh beet. Brown sliced onion in butter; add to the liquid. Season to taste. Bring to a boil. Serve with dumplings, *uszka*. Serves 6.
*Found in specialty food stores.

Rye Flour Kvas
Żur

2 cups rye flour

3 to 4 cups lukewarm water

Put the flour into a 1 1/2-quart crock and gradually add the water, stirring it into the flour until smooth. Cover the crock with a cloth and store in a warm place for 48 hours. The mixture will bubble. The kvas is done when brown liquid appears on the top. When you are ready to use it, skim off the foam. Add cold water to fill the crock, stirring it in. Allow the flour to settle for a few hours. Separate the clear liquid and refrigerate the clear liquid kvas in jars. Yields 3 cups.

White Borscht
Żurek

2 cups water
1 pound white Polish
   sausage
1 yellow onion, chopped
1 bay leaf
4 peppercorns

2 cups rye flour kvas (recipe
   on previous page)
2 garlic cloves
1 1/2 teaspoons marjoram
1/2 cup sour cream
salt and pepper

Combine the water with the sausage, onion, bay leaf, and peppercorns. Boil for 30 minutes. Remove the sausage, slice, and return to soup. Stir in the rye flour kvas and bring to a boil. Add garlic and marjoram and cook over very low heat for 10 minutes. Add the sour cream, salt and pepper. Serves 4 to 6.

Beef and Chicken Stock
Rosół

Henryka Woźniak

2 pounds beef with the bone
1/2 chicken
1 large carrot
2 parsley roots
1 stalk celery
1 medium-sized leek
1 yellow onion

4 cups chopped savoy
   cabbage
1 bay leaf
salt to taste
thyme to taste
5 peppercorns

Cover the meat with water and bring to boiling. Skim off the foam. Add the vegetables and spices. Continue boiling for another 30 minutes or until meat is tender. Remove from heat, cool, and remove the meat. Strain the broth and skim off the fat. Serve hot with noodles or dumplings. Perfect for a cold winter day. Serves 8. Note: This stock can be made using all chicken or all beef. It is a soup in itself or may be used as a base for another soup.

Cold Beet and
Cucumber Soup
Chłodnik

32-ounce bottle Manischewitz
    Borscht or 4 cups
    homemade borscht
1 quart buttermilk
3 tablespoons sour cream
1/2 cup finely chopped dill
1/2 cup finely chopped
    green onions

1/2 cup shredded radishes
1 cup peeled, seeded, and
    chopped cucumber
juice of 1/2 lemon
1/2 teaspoon salt
1/4 teaspoon pepper
2 hard-cooked eggs

Pour the borscht into a large bowl. Stir in the buttermilk and sour cream until smooth. Add the remaining ingredients except the eggs. Chill well. Serve in bowls and garnish each with a quarter of a hard-cooked egg. This is a perfect summer soup. Serves 8.

Mushroom Soup
Zupa Grzybowa

1 1/2 ounces dried mushrooms
2 yellow onions, chopped
1 pound beef with bone
1 3/4 quarts salted water
1 carrot

2 parsley roots
1 celery stalk
salt and pepper to taste
2 tablespoons sour cream
1 tablespoon parsley, chopped

Clean the mushrooms, add enough water to cover, and soak for 1 to 2 hours. Cook with the chopped onions, covered until tender. Strain and reserve the broth, remove the mushrooms, and slice. In a separate pot combine the cleaned meat and bones, and water. Cook slowly for 30 minutes. Add the vegetables and cook for another 30 minutes. Set aside to cool for 1 hour. Separate the broth and add it to the mushroom broth. Add the spices and mushrooms. Add the sour cream and garnish with chopped parsley. Serve hot. Serves 6 to 8.
Note: To make this without meat as a Christmas Eve soup, use 1/4 pound butter in place of the beef.

Dill Pickle Soup
Zupa Ogórkowa

Helen Pett
Allen Park, Michigan

8 cups rich chicken stock,
   homemade preferred
2 carrots, grated
2 cups pared and cubed
   potatoes
1 cup thinly sliced celery
5 large Polish dill pickles,
   coarsely grated

1/2 cup milk
2 tablespoons flour
1 egg
5 tablespoons sour cream
salt and pepper to taste
finely chopped parsley or
   fresh dill, optional
vinegar, optional

In a large pot, combine the stock, carrots, potatoes, and celery. Cook covered over low heat until the potatoes are soft, about 12 minutes. Add the pickles and cook for 15 minutes more. Combine the milk and flour and beat until smooth. Stir a small amount of the hot soup into flour mixture. Mix until smooth and return to soup, stirring well. Bring the soup to a boil, stirring frequently until the soup is slightly thick. Remove from heat. Beat the egg and sour cream until smooth. Pour a small amount of the hot soup into the sour cream mixture. Add to the soup and stir until smooth. Keep the soup warm but do not boil, or it will curdle. Add the salt and pepper to taste. Garnish with the dill or parsley. If you desire a soup that is sour, add about 1/4 cup vinegar. Serves 8.

Drawing by *Alice Wadowski-Bak*

Storks are a sign of good luck if they build a nest at your farm.

Duck Soup
Czernina

Shirley Ann Galanty
Dearborn Heights, Michigan

The soup was always a favorite when everyone came to Grandma's house for the Christmas holidays. When Grandma passed away, my mother continued the Czernina *tradition. After my mother's death, I quickly learned through trial and error to make it exactly like Grandma's and my mother's. This carried on family tradition and assured a good supply for my brothers, sisters, my own children, and many* Czernina *lovers who have been added to my Christmas list. Making* Czernina *has become a very satisfying Christmas project as well as a special gift.*

1 large duck (7 to 8 pounds) with double portion of blood	1 pound dried prunes, pitted
	1 cup raisins
	2 tablespoons flour
water	2 tablespoons sugar
2 tablespoons salt	16 to 24 ounces sour cream
2 teaspoons peppercorns	vinegar, sugar, and salt

Purchase the duck and blood from a poultry store. A container of blood mixed with vinegar will be given to you; ask for a double portion. Place the duck in a large kettle and cover with water. Add the salt and peppercorns; bring to a boil. Skim off the foam. Cover and cook until the meat is tender, about 2 hours. Remove the meat from bones and cut into pieces. Set aside. Add the raisins and prunes to stock. Cook 30 minutes. With beater blend the flour and sugar into the sour cream and beat until smooth. Add the blood a little at a time and continue beating. Slowly add a cup of the hot soup stock to the blood mixture, blending thoroughly. Pour the blood mixture into stock stirring constantly until the soup comes to a boil. Season to taste with additional vinegar, sugar, and salt. Return the meat to the soup. Serve with homemade noodles, boiled potatoes or both. Makes about 3 quarts.

Note: For thicker soup increase the flour to 4 to 6 tablespoons or add 1 cup pureed prunes. Soup can be stored in refrigerator for a week or it can be frozen. When reheating, if the soup appears too thick, add a little water.

Easter Soup
Biały Barszcz

Mary C. Gorecki
Pennington, New Jersey

1 loaf rye bread
boiling water
2 1/2 teaspoons salt
1 3/4 teaspoons pepper
1 1/2 teaspoons sour salt
    (citric acid)*
1 cup sour cream
2 cups cubed roast beef
2 cups cubed roast pork

2 cups thinly sliced baked
    kielbasa, smoked or fresh
2 cups cubed cooked ham
Easter Cheese, sliced, recipe
    found on page 117
12 hard-cooked eggs, diced
4- to 5-inch piece of horse-
    radish root, scraped with
    a knife

Place the loaf of bread in a 2-gallon crock and fill the crock with boiling water. Cover with cheesecloth and allow to sit for 2 to 3 days, until it sours. Strain the liquid and refrigerate liquid. On serving day, place the liquid in a 6-quart pot and add the salt, pepper, and sour salt. Bring to a boil, reduce heat to low, and add the sour cream. Simmer so the sour cream does not curdle. Add the meats, cheese, and hard-cooked eggs. Add the horseradish. Season to taste. Heat and serve hot in bowl. Everyone wants seconds. Can be frozen in containers and savored in the weeks that follow. Makes about 1 1/2 gallons.
*Available in drug stores.

Polish Cold Soup with Shrimp
Chłodnik

Ronald S. Nowak
Sales Director
Polish Union of America
Buffalo, New York

1 small bunch firm young
    beets, peeled and grated
1 1/2 quarts cold water
3 tablespoons red wine
    vinegar, divided
5 teaspoons salt, divided
1 1/2 teaspoons sugar, divided
1 pound uncooked shrimp
    (or crayfish tails in season)
1 cup sour cream
2 medium-sized cucumbers,
    peeled, seeded, and diced
4 medium-sized scallions,
    including 2 inches of the
    green tops, sliced

4 red radishes, thinly sliced
4 tablespoons finely chopped
    fresh dill leaves or 4
    teaspoons dried dill weed,
    divided
3 tablespoons strained fresh
    lemon juice
pinch white pepper
1 lemon, thinly sliced, for
    garnish
3 hard-cooked eggs, chilled
    and finely chopped, for
    garnish

Bring the grated beets and cold water to a boil over high heat in a 3- to 4-quart enameled or stainless-steel saucepan. Reduce heat to moderate and cook uncovered for 1 minute. Reduce heat to low, stir in 2 tablespoons of the vinegar, 2 teaspoons of the salt and 1 teaspoon of the sugar; simmer partially covered for 30 minutes. Drain the beets. Set the beets and cooking liquid aside, separately, to cool to room temperature. Peel, devein, and wash the shrimp under cold water. Then bring 1 quart of water to a boil in a small pan, drop in the shrimp and cook briskly, uncovered, for about 3 minutes, or until they turn pink and are firm to the touch. Drain and coarsely chop the shrimp. Set aside to cool. When the beet cooking liquid is completely cooled, beat in the sour cream with a wire whisk. Stir in the beets, shrimp, cucumbers, scallions, radishes, 2 tablespoons of the fresh dill or two teaspoons of dried dill, the lemon juice, remaining vinegar, salt, sugar and white pepper. Taste for seasoning, cover the bowl tightly with plastic wrap, and refrigerate for at least 3 hours, or until the *chłodnik* is thoroughly chilled. To serve, ladle the soup into a large chilled tureen or individual soup plates. Sprinkle the remaining dill on top and, if you like, garnish the *chłodnik* with thin slices of lemon and chopped hard-cooked eggs. Serves 8.

Barley Soup
Krupnik-Zupa

1/2 cup barley	1 large white potato, diced
1 1/2 quarts beef broth	2 tablespoons chopped parsley for garnish

Clean the barley and soak in water for 3 hours. Boil the beef broth for 15 minutes. Add the barley and cook for 30 minutes. Add the potato and cook for 10 more minutes. Serve hot, garnished with parsley. Serves 6.

Prune Soup
Zupa Śliwkowa

12 ounces pitted dried prunes	1 tablespoon sugar
2 ounces dried apples	3 tablespoons sour cream
1 quart water	2 teaspoons lemon juice

Combine the dried fruits, water, and sugar. Cook for 15 minutes. Set aside for 3 to 5 hours. Place the mixture into a blender, add the sour cream and lemon juice, and blend until smooth. Serve hot or cold. Serves 4.

Blueberry Soup
Zupa z Czarnych Jagód

3 tablespoons sugar
1/2 cup water
2 pints blueberries

1 cup sour cream
1/2 cup white wine

Bring sugar and water to a boil and add blueberries. Cook until the blueberries pop. Press this mixture through a sieve and cool. Add sour cream and wine. Serve cold. Serves 4.

Vegetable Soup
Zupa Jarzynowa

Henryka Woźniak

1 1/2 quarts water or meat
   stock
1/2 onion, sliced
1 leek, sliced
1 carrot, sliced
1 small cauliflower, cut into
   flowerets
1 parsley root, sliced
1 stalk celery, sliced
1 potato, cubed

6 ounces string beans, cut into
   1-inch pieces
6 ounces green peas
2 tomatoes, peeled and
   quartered
1 tablespoon butter
1 teaspoon flour
1 tablespoon chopped dill or
   parsley

Combine the meat stock with the onion, leek, carrot, cauliflower, parsley root, and celery. Cook 15 minutes over low heat. Add the potato, string beans, peas, and tomatoes. Simmer for another 10 minutes. In another pan, melt the butter, sprinkle in the flour, and stir until smooth. Add the butter mixture to the soup. Bring to a boil. Garnish with chopped dill and parsley. Serves 6 to 8.

Beer Stew
Gulasz na Piwie

Maria Ganowska
Chicago, Illinois

2 pounds pork, cut into
   1-inch cubes
3 tablespoons margarine
2 onions, cut into quarters
3 white peppercorns
1/2 teaspoon thyme

1 bay leaf
1/2 cup beef broth or water
1/2 cup beer
1/2 cup white wine
salt and pepper to taste

In a large skillet brown the meat in margarine. Remove the meat from the pan. Brown the onions in the same skillet, then return the meat to the pan. Add the spices and broth; simmer for 45 minutes. Add the beer and wine and bring to a boil. Serve with whole potatoes or noodles. Serves 4.

Polish-born Marian Owczarski creates stainless steel sculpture as artist-in-residence at Orchard Lake Schools. His works are in public and private collections in the United States, Europe, and Canada.

Sauerkraut Soup
Kapuśniak

2 pounds pork shank or
   pigs' feet
1 quart water
1 pound sauerkraut
1 bay leaf

5 peppercorns
3 white peppercorns
6 ounces bacon
2 onions, sliced
1 tablespoon flour

Cook the pork shanks in the water for an hour. Skim off the foam. Remove the meat from broth. Discard the skin and bones. Dice the meat and return to the pot. Add the sauerkraut, bay leaf, and peppercorns, and cook for another hour. Fry the bacon until golden; remove from fat, and add to the soup. Remove half of the bacon grease from the frying pan and fry the onions until golden. Sprinkle with the flour and stir until smooth. Add to the soup. Cook over low heat for 5 minutes. Add salt and pepper to taste. Serves 6.

Tomato Soup
Zupa Pomidorowa

Henryka Woźniak

8 cups chicken or beef broth
1 large parsley root
1 carrot
1 celery stalk
1 leek
5 small parsley sprigs

1 small onion
1 small can tomato paste
1/4 teaspoon flour dissolved
   in 3 tablespoons of water
salt and pepper to taste
sour cream

Clean the vegetables. Combine the broth with the vegetables and cook for about 60 minutes. Cool the vegetable broth and discard the vegetables. Dissolve the tomato paste in the broth. Bring to boil and simmer for 3 minutes. Add the flour mixture, stirring in well. Season to taste. Serve in small bowls with 1 teaspoon of sour cream in each. Can be served with cooked rice or noodles in the soup. Serves 8.

Salads

Vegetable Salad
Sałatka Jarzynowa

Henryka Woźniak

2 medium-sized white
    potatoes
3 medium-sized carrots
1/2 celery root
1 medium-sized parsley root
3 hard-cooked eggs
2 dill pickles, diced
2 apples, diced

1 can green peas, (4-ounce
    can)
1 leek, diced
1/2 cup mayonnaise
1/2 cup sour cream
1 tablespoon Dijon mustard
salt and pepper to taste

Garnish:
tomatoes
marinated red bell pepper

parsley

Boil unpared potatoes, carrots, celery and parsley roots in salted water. When tender, remove the peels, and finely dice the vegetables and eggs. Add the pickles, apples, peas, and leek. Set aside. Combine the remaining ingredients. Pour over the diced vegetables and mix thoroughly. Chill. Serve garnished with tomato halves, slices of marinated red pepper and parsley. Serves 4 to 6.

Leek Salad
Sałatka z Porów

1 leek, sliced
1 apple, peeled and shredded
juice of 1/2 lemon

2 teaspoons sugar
salt and pepper to taste
mayonnaise to taste

Combine all the ingredients. Toss to coat with the mayonnaise. Refrigerate for 1 to 2 hours. Serves 2.

Sauerkraut Salad
Surówka z Kiszonej Kapusty

Lila Lam-Nowakowska
Kraków, Poland

1/4 cup salad or olive oil
1 tablespoon sugar
1 teaspoon caraway seeds,
   optional
1/2 teaspoon salt

1 pound sauerkraut, rinsed,
   drained and chopped
2 tart apples, peeled, cored
   and diced
3/4 cup grated carrots

Combine the oil, sugar and spices. Stir the sauerkraut into the oil mixture. Add the apples and carrots. Toss to coat. Good with fried fish. Serves 4.

Celery Root Salad
Sałatka z Selera

1 large celery root
pepper to taste
1 tablespoon sour cream

2 tablespoons mayonnaise
salt and pepper to taste
1 ounce walnuts, chopped

Grate the celery root and sprinkle with pepper. Set aside for ten minutes. Combine the sour cream and mayonnaise; add the salt and pepper to taste. Pour the sour cream mixture over the celery and mix thoroughly. Add the nuts and serve. Serves 4.
Note: Celery root is available in specialty shops. It is in season in September and early October.

Pisanki *from Huculi in the Carpathian mountains were created before World War II by Polish villagers whose village was destroyed. These* pisanki *are in the Polish Museum of America, Chicago, Illinois.*

Cucumbers in Sour Cream
Mizeria ze Śmietaną

Virginia Luty
Hinckley, Ohio

3 cups sliced cucumbers
salt to taste
1/4 cup fresh dill or
   2 tablespoons dried dill

1 cup dairy sour cream or
   yogurt

Sprinkle the cucumbers with salt. Let stand for 30 minutes; pat dry with paper towels. In a bowl, stir the dill into sour cream. Add the cucumbers and mix well. Serves 4 to 6.

Red Cabbage Salad
Sałatka z Czerwonej Kapusty

2-pound head red cabbage,
   finely shredded
juice of 1/2 lemon
1 small red onion, finely
   chopped
2 tart apples, shredded

1 tablespoon sugar
1 teaspoon salt
1 tablespoon olive oil
pepper
1 tablespoon chopped parsley

Boil the cabbage for a few minutes; drain. The cabbage will become violet. Sprinkle with the lemon juice and watch the cabbage become red. Add the remaining ingredients except the parsley, and toss. Refrigerate for 3 hours. Garnish with parsley. Serves 6.

Breads

Yeast Bread
Ciasto Drożdżowe

Lila Lam-Nowakowska

For Easter the bread is baked with a cross on the top.

1 1/2 ounces yeast
1 tablespoon warm milk
1/4 cup sugar, divided
4 cups flour, divided
2 eggs, separated

1 teaspoon salt
grated lemon rind
1 1/2 cups milk
1/4 cup butter, melted

Dissolve the yeast in warm milk; add a teaspoon of sugar and 1 teaspoon of flour. Beat the egg yolks and the remaining sugar until light. Put the remaining flour into a large bowl. Make a well in the flour. Pour the yeast mixture into well; cover with flour. Wait for the yeast to grow. If it doesn't, add more yeast. Add the egg yolk mixture, salt and lemon rind; mix well. Add the milk gradually. Knead the dough for about 5 minutes and add the melted butter, blending it through the dough. Put the dough into a greased loaf pan and cover. Let rise for 2 to 3 hours. Brush the dough with the egg whites, lightly beaten. Bake at 350° for 50 minutes. Test for doneness with a toothpick. If it comes out dry, the bread is done.

Wycinanki *by Alice Wadowski-Bak*

Sourdough Starter

1 package dry yeast	2 cups flour
2 1/2 cups warm water, divided	1 tablespoon sugar

Soften the yeast in 1/2 cup warm water. Add the remaining water, flour and sugar and beat until smooth. Place in a large glass or ceramic bowl. Do not use a metal bowl. Cover with cheesecloth or a towel and let stand in a warm place until it begins to bubble, about 24 to 48 hours. Discard and start over if signs of fermentation have not begun. Stir well, cover and let stand several days or until the mixture becomes foamy. Stir well and place in a glass jar. Cover and refrigerate. When the liquid rises to the top, starter is ready to use. Stir well before using. Replenish by adding 1 cup water and 1 cup flour. Store in refrigerator.

Polish Rye Bread

1 package dry yeast	3 tablespoons butter, or
1 1/2 cups warm water	shortening, or bacon fat
3 cups rye flour	2 teaspoons salt
1 cup Sourdough Starter	3 to 3 1/4 cups flour, divided
at room temperature	1/2 teaspoon baking soda
1/4 cup sugar	

In a large bowl soften the yeast in the water. Blend in the rye flour, starter, sugar, butter and salt. Beat well. Combine 1 cup of flour with soda and stir into the yeast mixture. Add enough remaining flour to make a moderately stiff dough. Knead on a floured board about 5 to 8 minutes. Place the dough in a greased bowl, turning once. Cover and let rise until double, about 1 1/2 hours. Punch the dough down, divide in half. Cover and let rest 10 minutes. Shape into 2 loaves and place in greased 8x4-inch loaf pans. Let rise until almost double, about 45 minutes. Bake at 375° for 30 to 40 minutes. Remove from pans immediately and cool on rack.

Buckwheat Groats

Jenny Ramczyk
Polish Museum
Winona, Minnesota

9 cups water
1 pound buckwheat groats
7 to 8 medium-sized potatoes, grated

4 teaspoons salt
1/2 cup bacon grease
butter

Bring the water to a boil. Add the groats and potatoes. Turn off heat. Let stand for 10 minutes. Turn heat back on to medium. Add the salt and bacon grease. Stir and cook until the buckwheat is soft. Place in a 5x9-inch loaf pan and chill. When cold, slice into pieces 1/3 inch thick. Fry in the butter until brown and crispy. Serve hot with butter, syrup or plain. Serves 12.

Whole Wheat Bread

Polish Museum
Winona, Minnesota

3 cups warm water
1/4 cup honey
1 cup milk
1 package dry yeast
1 tablespoon salt

1 egg, beaten
3 1/2 cups whole wheat flour
3 1/2 cups white flour
butter

Combine the water, honey, and milk. Dissolve the yeast in water mixture. Set aside for 10 minutes. Add the salt and egg. Add the flours one cup at a time until you have a soft dough. Turn the dough onto a smooth, floured surface and knead for 5 to 10 minutes until the dough is smooth and elastic. Wash the bowl and grease with butter. Place the dough in bowl and turn it once to grease top. Let rise for 3 hours. Punch the dough down and divide into 2 loaves. Place in 5x9-inch loaf pans and let rise for 30 minutes. Place the dough in a cold oven and bake at 375° for 40 to 60 minutes.

Main Dishes

Helen Pett, volunteer, cooks pierogi *for the Polish Falcons of America #79, Detroit, Michigan.*

Pierogi

2 cups flour
1/2 cup water
1 whole egg
1 egg yolk

2 tablespoons sour cream
1/2 teaspoon salt
1 teaspoon butter or margarine

If you have a dough hook, mix all ingredients until the dough is pliable. Or mix the ingredients together with a spoon and then knead. If the dough is too soft, add more flour; if too stiff, add water. Cut the dough in half and roll out to 1/16th of an inch thick. Cut into circles about 3 1/2 inches in diameter. Place a spoonful of your favorite filling on half the circle. Fold over and press the edges together. If the dough won't seal, put some water on the edge of the circle and pinch together. Put the pierogi into boiling salted water. Cook 5 minutes. Remove from water with a slotted spoon and serve with melted butter. Or cook the pierogi in butter until lightly browned. Pierogi can be filled with potato, cheese, mushroom, plum, sauerkraut, or cherry fillings.

Pierogi Fillings

Potato Filling:

1 medium-sized onion,
    chopped fine
butter
2 cups mashed potatoes, hot

salt and pepper
1/2 cup grated sharp
    Cheddar cheese

Sauté the onion in butter until golden. Combine all the ingredients and shape into potato balls, place on the dough and complete as directed. Serves 4.

Cheese Filling:

farmer's cheese or
    dry cottage cheese
salt and pepper

finely chopped green onions
    to taste

Combine all the ingredients and use to fill pierogi.

Plum Filling :

1 large can pitted plums

Wrap the plums in pierogi dough.

Sauerkraut Filling:

1 can (10-ounce) sauerkraut
1 small onion, chopped fine

1 tablespoon butter
salt and pepper

Cook the sauerkraut for about 20 minutes. Rinse in cold water and squeeze dry. Sauté the onion in butter and add to the sauerkraut. Add the salt and pepper and fill the pierogi. Serves 4.

Cheese and Potato Filling:

1 1/2 cups mashed potatoes,
    made with about
    2 tablespoons butter

1 1/2 cups dry cottage cheese
2 to 4 large onions, minced
salt and pepper to taste

Combine all the ingredients and mix well. Let cool and fill the pierogi with desired amount. Serves 4.

Beef Slices
Zrazy Zawijane

Lila Lam-Nowakowska
Kraków, Poland

2 pounds beef eye of round, top round or sirloin, cut in thin steaks
salt and pepper
1 sweet pickle, cut lengthwise into six wedges
5 slices bacon, cut into small pieces
1 onion, sliced
1/2 cup all-purpose flour
1 teaspoon salt
1/2 teaspoon pepper
3 tablespoons butter or other fat
1/2 cup sour cream

Pound the meat. Sprinkle with salt and pepper. Let it stand for 30 minutes. Pound the meat again until thin. Roll a piece of pickle, bacon and onion into each slice of beef. Secure with a toothpick. Combine the flour, salt and pepper. Coat each roll with the flour mixture. Brown each roll on all sides in the butter over high heat. Add 1/2 cup water and simmer about 60 minutes. Blend 3 table-spoons of the juices from the pan with the sour cream until smooth. Add the sour cream mixture to the meat. Bring to a boil and simmer for 5 minutes. Serve with noodles or boiled buckwheat. Serves 4.

Performing with the Syrena Dance Ensemble of the Polish Roman Catholic Union of America are, from left, James Steven and Jack Marchewka of Dearborn Heights and Evan Demers of Northville, Michigan. They are in the Krakowiak costume from Kraków.

Hunter's Stew
Bigos

Henryka Woźniak

The best bigos cooks are hunters, hence the name. It is a very popular dish during hunting expeditions.

1 pound pork bones
2 pounds sauerkraut,
   drained and rinsed
3/4 pound cabbage, chopped
4 large yellow onions, divided
2 white peppercorns
2 bay leaves, divided
1 ounce dried mushrooms,
   divided
1 pound pork butt or fat ham,
   cubed

3/4 pound beef, cubed
1 tablespoon lard
1 teaspoon salt
5 black peppercorns, divided
4 slices bacon
1/2 pound smoked sausage
2 tablespoons flour
1 teaspoon marjoram
1 bouillon cube, crushed
3/4 cup red wine

Cook the bones in 4 cups of water for 2 hours until you get stock. Put the sauerkraut into a large pot. Add the cabbage. Cover the sauerkraut mixture with stock. Chop 2 onions and add to the kraut. Add the white peppercorns, one bay leaf and half the mushrooms. Simmer 1 1/2 hours. Meanwhile, brown the pork and beef in the lard; add the salt, black pepper, a bay leaf and remaining mushrooms. Cut the remaining onions into rings and add to the meat. Simmer until the meat is tender, adding 2 tablespoons of water every 15 minutes. Cool and dice into 1/2-inch pieces. Fry the bacon and remove from pan when done. Cut the sausage into small rounds and add to the bacon grease in the pan. Cook until done. Remove sausage from pan. Add flour to bacon fat; stir until smooth. Add the marjoram, crushed bouillon cube and red wine. Add the gravy to sauerkraut. Combine the meat, sausage, and kraut mixture. Crumble the bacon in. Simmer this mixture for about 2 hours. This dish is best prepared at least a week in advance and simmered 1/2 hour before serving. Serves 6.

Ground Meat Cutlet
Kotlet Mielony or *Sznycel*

There is a regional difference over the name of this dish. In Central and Northern Poland it is called Kotlet Mielony. *In Southern Poland it is called* Sznycel. *Northerners say that* Schnitzel, *the original word for the southern version of the name, is a sophisticated type of meat, while ground cutlets are a very ordinary food, and trying to name this dish after a "noble meat" is a sign of bad taste. Similar reasoning has Poles from the south stating that the cutlet is one of the prime meats. All arguments aside, this is one of the most popular dishes in Poland, just as hamburger is in the United States.*

2 dried bread rolls	3 eggs
1 pound ground beef	salt and pepper to taste
1 pound ground pork	2 cloves garlic, crushed
2 large yellow onions, finely chopped	1/2 cup bread crumbs
	2 tablespoons oil or lard

Soak the dried rolls in water. Remove from the water and squeeze dry. Combine the rolls, ground meats, onion, eggs, spices and garlic. Mix thoroughly and form into small ovals, like hamburgers. Dip the patties into the bread crumbs. Heat the oil in a frying pan and fry the cutlets in the oil until brown and cooked through. Serve hot with potatoes or boiled buckwheat. Serves 6.

This contemporary church in Doylestown, Pennsylvania, houses a copy of the painting of the Black Madonna of Częstochowa, as well as stained glass windows depicting the religious histories of the United States and Poland.

Calf Liver
Wątróbka Cielęca

Jerzy Kazimierski
Chicago, Illinois

Jerzy was at one time a prominent lawyer in Warsaw. He is an excellent cook and now works for several families in the United States.

1 pound calf liver
2 cups skim milk or 1 cup whole
    milk and 1 cup water
2 medium-sized onions, sliced

4 tablespoons margarine,
    divided
1 tablespoon chopped parsley
salt and pepper to taste

Soak the calf liver in the milk for 2 to 3 hours. Remove and pat dry with a paper towel. Sauté the onions in 2 tablespoons of margarine until golden. Set aside. Slice the calf liver. Brown the slices in the remaining margarine, 1 to 2 minutes per side. Cover the slices with the prepared onions and heat for 3 minutes. Sprinkle with salt and pepper and garnish with parsley. Serve hot with mashed potatoes. Serves 2 to 3.

Baked Pheasant
Bażant Pieczony

Jerzy Kazimierski

1 whole pheasant, cleaned
2 teaspoons salt
1/2 teaspoon pepper

6 slices bacon
1/2 cup chicken broth

Preheat the oven to 350°. Sprinkle the pheasant with salt and pepper. Wrap it with the bacon strips and tie with cooking twine. Bake the pheasant for 45 minutes, basting often. Remove the pheasant from oven and unwrap. Increase oven temperature to 550°. Sprinkle the chicken broth over the pheasant and return to oven for another 5 minutes, or until golden. Serve with potatoes or rice. Serves 4.

Veal Kidneys
Nerkówka Cielęca

Jerzy Kazimierski

3 pounds veal kidneys
1/4 cup oil
1 cup chicken broth
4 medium-sized tomatoes,
   peeled and quartered

1/2 cup white wine
Madeira to taste, optional
salt and pepper to taste

Clean the kidneys, removing fatty parts. Tie the kidneys together with thread and brown on all sides in the oil. When browned, reduce heat and add broth. Simmer covered until tender. Add the remaining ingredients and continue cooking for 5 more minutes. Remove the kidneys from the pan, slice and serve with the sauce. Serves 6. Perfect with potatoes and grilled mushrooms.

Mixed Meats in a Fresh Pepper Sauce
Paprykarz

Malgorzata Nowakowski

1 pound each meat: beef,
   veal, and pork, cut into
   1-inch cubes
2 tablespoons flour
2 tablespoons vegetable oil
3 onions, cut in quarters
2 green peppers, cut in
   squares, divided

2 cups beef broth
salt and pepper to taste
1 teaspoon dried red pepper
1 bay leaf
1 clove garlic, minced
3 tomatoes, cut in quarters
1/2 cup sour cream, optional

Coat the meats with flour, then brown in oil. Remove from pan and set aside. In the same skillet brown onions. Add meat to onions, along with 1/2 of the prepared green peppers, broth, salt, pepper, dried red pepper, bay leaf, and garlic. Simmer for about 45 minutes. Add remaining green peppers and cook all together for another 15 minutes. Add the tomatoes 5 minutes before serving. Blend sour cream into the sauce, if desired. Serve with noodles.

Stuffed Cabbage Rolls
Gołąbki

Helen Kujawski
Fenton, Michigan

1 head cabbage	1/2 teaspoon salt
1 cup uncooked rice	1/2 teaspoon pepper
1 onion, chopped fine	1/2 teaspoon garlic powder
2 teaspoons butter	4 slices bacon
1 pound ground beef	2 10 1/2-ounce cans tomato
1/2 pound ground pork	soup
1 egg	

Remove the core from the whole head of cabbage with a sharp knife. Scald the cabbage in boiling water. Remove a few leaves at a time as they wilt. Place the rice in 1 cup of water and boil 10 minutes. Sauté the onions in butter until partly browned. Combine with the rice, meat, egg, salt, pepper, and garlic powder; mix well. Shave off part of the cabbage leaf stem for easier rolling. Place the meat mixture on the stem of leaf and roll over once, put side ends of the cabbage leaf in and finish rolling. If needed fasten with toothpick. To cook, place the slices of bacon with a few cabbage leaves and any leftover small leaves at the bottom of the baking dish. Place the rolls on top, cover with the tomato soup and cover with any remaining cabbage leaves. Cover with a lid or foil and bake about 2 to 2 1/2 hours at 300°. Serves 6.

Wycinanki *by folk artist Ryszarda Klim of Milwaukee, Wisconsin.*

Beef Stroganoff

Chef from Orbit Restaurant
Chicago, Illinois

1 tablespoon flour
salt, pepper and dried red
   pepper to taste
2 pounds beef eye of round or
   sirloin, cut in thin slices
2 tablespoons butter or lard

2 yellow onions, sliced
1/2 pound mushrooms, sliced
1 cup beef broth
2 tablespoons tomato paste
1 cup sour cream
1 tablespoon chopped parsley

Mix the flour, salt, pepper, and red pepper together and use to coat the meat. In a large skillet brown the meat in butter. Remove meat and set aside. In the same skillet, sauté the onions and then the mushrooms. Combine the meat, onions, and mushrooms in a large pan. Add the beef broth and tomato paste and simmer for about 30 minutes. Stirring constantly, add the sour cream and bring to a boil. Sprinkle with parsley. Serve with egg drops. Serves 6.

Polish Noodles
and Cabbage

Pat Graczyk
Garden City, Michigan

1/4 cup butter or margarine
1/2 cup chopped onions
4 cups chopped or sliced
   cabbage
1 teaspoon caraway seed

1/2 teaspoon salt
1/8 teaspoon pepper
1 package (8 ounces) egg
   noodles
1/2 cup sour cream, optional

Melt the butter in large skillet, add the onions; sauté until soft. Add the cabbage, sauté 5 minutes or until crisp-tender. Stir in the caraway seed, salt, and pepper. Cook the noodles in boiling salted water, drain well. Stir the noodles into the cabbage; add the sour cream. Cook 5 minutes longer, stirring frequently. Serves 6.

Stuffed Cabbage

Erica Farris
Polish Roman Catholic Union of America
Livonia, Michigan

8 pounds cabbage, in
   medium-sized heads
2 cups finely chopped onion
1/2 pound butter, divided
2 cups rice
2 pounds ground beef
2 pounds ground pork
3 eggs

1 tablespoon salt
3/4 teaspoon pepper
1 package dry onion soup mix,
   divided
butter
1 can (48-ounce) chicken broth
1 quart sour cream, divided

Core the cabbage heads, scald in boiling water. Separate the leaves and remove the remaining hard core of each leaf. Sauté the onion in 1/4 pound butter, to a golden brown. Do not burn! In another pan barely cover the rice with water. Bring to a boil; cover the pan and let stand until cool. Mix the meat, eggs, salt, pepper, cooled rice, and onions well. Spread the meat mixture in a mound in the center of each cabbage leaf. Fold sides over toward center, then roll up. Line roasting pan with smaller, leftover cabbage leaves. Layer the cabbage rolls in the pan and cover with a layer of cabbage leaves. Sprinkle with a little salt and pepper and half the package of the onion soup mix. Dot with butter. Repeat with a layer of cabbage rolls and cover with the remaining cabbage leaves. Again season with a little salt and pepper and 1/2 package of onion soup mix. Dot with butter. Pour the chicken broth over the rolls to one inch from the top of pan. Cover and bake at 350° for approximately 2 to 2 1/2 hours. The top layer of cabbage leaves will start to brown. In a bowl gradually add some of the hot broth to 1 pint of the sour cream. Blend thoroughly and pour over the cabbage rolls. Baste carefully so that all of the broth is well-mixed with the sour cream. Bake 1/2 hour longer, until bubbly. The cabbage is ready for serving. However, for better flavor, cook one day ahead. Refrigerate until ready to serve. Then mix the broth with another pint of sour cream, return to oven and bake the rolls at 350° until hot for about 2 hours. Serves 10. Yield: 30 cabbage rolls.

Polish Sausage
Smothered
in Red Cabbage

1 small head cabbage
vinegar or fresh lemon juice
1 tablespoon butter
1 1/2 teaspoons flour
1 cup dry red wine or strong
    broth

1 1/2 teaspoons instant
    bouillon
salt and pepper
sugar and lemon juice to taste
1 ring smoked Polish sausage

Shred the cabbage. Place in boiling water for 3 minutes, drain, and sprinkle with the vinegar or lemon juice to restore color. Melt the butter in a heavy skillet; blend in flour. Gradually add the wine or broth. Heat, stirring until thickened and smooth. Add the cabbage, instant bouillon, salt, pepper, sugar, and lemon juice. Cover and simmer 30 minutes. Add the sausage and continue to cook for 20 minutes, until the sausage is tender. Serves 2 to 4.

Polish Hot Pot

Kowalski Sausage Company
Hamtramck, Mich.

6 large potatoes
1/2 pound Polish sausage or
    bologna
6 onions, sliced thick

1 can (1 pound) tomatoes
1 1/2 teaspoons paprika
1 teaspoon salt
1/2 cup sour cream

Pare the potatoes and cut into 1/2-inch slices. Arrange in the bottom of a large greased casserole. Cut the sausage into 1 or 2-inch cubes and place over potatoes. Top with thick onion slices. Combine the tomatoes, paprika and salt; add to the casserole. Bake at 350° for 45 minutes. Stir in the sour cream and bake 15 minutes longer. Makes 6 servings.

Carp in Aspic
Karp w Galarecie

Henryka Woźniak

1 whole carp, well-gutted and
    scaled, with head removed
1 carrot
2 sprigs parsley
1/4 medium-sized celery
    root
1 leek
1 yellow onion
1 bay leaf
8 peppercorns
1 white peppercorn
1 envelope unflavored
    gelatin, if needed

Boil all the vegetables and spices for 10 minutes in water to cover. Cut the prepared carp into 1-inch slices. Add the pieces and the carp head to the vegetables and boil for 20 minutes. Remove the fish and vegetables with a slotted spoon. Debone the fish and place in a mold or bowl; garnish with the vegetables. Check to see if liquid has become aspic; if it is not stiff, add gelatin. To add the gelatin, soften in 1/4 cup cold water. Place over hot water to dissolve. Add to the hot fish liquid. Pour over the fish. Refrigerate until set. Serve cold. Serves 4 to 6.

Carp

1 whole carp, well-gutted and
    scaled; head removed
salt and pepper to taste
4 to 5 whole cloves, crushed
2 tablespoons white vinegar
2 onions, sliced
1/4 cup butter
1/2 cup beer
1 1/2 ounces white raisins
1/2 teaspoon grated lemon
    rind
chopped parsley

Cut the carp into 1-inch slices. Sprinkle the slices with salt, pepper, cloves and vinegar. Set aside. Sauté the onions in butter until translucent. Add the beer and heat. Add the fish and simmer, covered, for 30 minutes. When the fish flakes, remove fish and onion with a slotted spoon. Add the raisins and lemon rind to sauce. Place the fish on a serving platter. Cover with sauce and garnish with chopped parsley. Serves 4.

Warsaw-style Tripe
Flaki po Warszawsku

2 pounds fresh tripe
1 pound veal bones
salt and pepper
2 carrots, sliced
3 stalks celery, sliced
1 onion, chopped
1 tablespoon fresh parsley,
   chopped

1/4 teaspoon ginger
1/4 teaspoon mace
2 teaspoons marjoram
2 cups meat broth
2 tablespoons butter or
   margarine
1 tablespoon flour
1/2 cup light cream

Rinse the tripe thoroughly with cold water. In a large kettle combine the tripe and veal bones with enough water to cover. Add salt and pepper. Bring to a boil, reduce heat, and cook 4 to 5 hours, or until the tripe is tender. Drain the tripe; discard the bones and cooking liquid. Cut the tripe into very thin strips. Cook the strips with vegetables and spices in the broth until the vegetables are tender. Melt the butter in a pan and stir in the flour until smooth and golden. Blend in a small amount of the cooking liquid from the tripe. Add salt and pepper. Add the cream gradually. Drain the vegetables and tripe. Stir into sauce. Simmer another 5 minutes. Serves 4 to 6.

Woodcarvings by Henry A. Wicks are included among exhibits at the Polish Museum, Winona, Minnesota.

147

Greek-style Fish
Ryba po Grecku

1 pound carp or whitefish
    fillets
salt and pepper
5 tablespoons olive oil,
    divided
1 cup chopped onion
1/2 cup sliced celery
1/2 cup shredded carrots

1/2 cup chopped parsley
1/2 cup chicken broth or
    water
6 ounces tomato paste
1 bay leaf
1/2 teaspoon sugar
1 teaspoon lemon juice

Cut the fish fillets into 2-inch pieces. Sprinkle the fish with salt. Fry the fish in 3 tablespoons olive oil. Arrange the cooked fish in a casserole and keep warm. Sauté the chopped onion in the remaining oil. Add all the vegetables, chicken broth, tomato paste, and bay leaf; simmer mixture for 15 minutes. Add the sugar, salt, lemon juice, and pepper to taste. Pour the vegetable mixture over fish. Place in a preheated 350° oven for 10 minutes. Serves 4.

Herring in Oil
Śledź w Oleju

Henryka Woźniak

4 salted herring
1/4 cup wine vinegar, divided
2 yellow onions, chopped

1/2 cup olive oil
1/2 cup chopped green onions

Soak the herring in water for 24 hours, changing water after the first 6 hours. Drain the herring. Remove the skin and bones. Cut the herring into 1-inch slices. Place slices on a serving dish. Sprinkle them on both sides with half of the vinegar. Arrange the chopped yellow onions around fish. Pour the oil and remaining vinegar over the fish. Garnish with green onions. Prepare at least 1 hour before serving. Serves 6 to 8.

Marinated Herring
Śledź Marynowany

This dish is very popular for Shrovetide.

2 salted herring	2 white peppercorns
1 cup water	3 black peppercorns
1 onion, thinly sliced	1 cup vinegar
2 bay leaves	2 teaspoons sugar

Soak the herring in cold water for 24 hours, changing the water after the first 6 hours. Clean the herring, remove the skin and bones, cut lengthwise. Place the herring in a jar. Boil the water, onion, and spices together. Cool and add the vinegar and sugar. Pour the mixture over the herring. Cover the jar and set aside for 24 to 48 hours. Serves 4.

Herring in Sour Cream with Onion and Apple
Śledź w Śmietanie z
Cebulą i Jabłkiem

Henryka Woźniak

1 salted herring	1/2 cup sour cream
1 tablespoon vegetable oil	1/2 teaspoon sugar
1/2 cup white wine vinegar	1 tablespoon mayonnaise
1 yellow onion, thinly sliced	2 tablespoons chopped
1 apple, peeled and sliced	parsley

Clean the herring and soak in cold water for 24 hours, changing the water after the first 6 hours. Clean the herring again, remove skin. Fillet the herring, removing the bones. Cut into 1-inch cubes. Sprinkle with oil and vinegar; set aside for 2 hours. Meanwhile, blanch the onion slices in boiling water. Drain and cool. Combine the onion and apple. Cover each piece of herring with the onion-apple mixture. Combine the sour cream, sugar, and mayonnaise; pour over the herring. Garnish with parsley. Serves 2 to 4.

Pork Roast with Prunes
Schab Pieczony ze Śliwkami

Malgorzata Nowakowski

This roast is popular in many Eastern and Central European countries.

1 pork loin roast, about 4
  pounds
1 pound pitted prunes
1/4 teaspoon cinnamon
1 tablespoon marjoram

salt and pepper to taste
2 tablespoons butter, melted
1 cup hot water
1 chicken bouillon cube

With a long sharp knife, make a hole through the center of the loin. Stuff the prunes in the hole. Combine spices. Rub the roast with spice mixture and set aside for 3 to 4 hours. Place the butter in the hot water; add chicken bouillon cube. Stir until dissolved. Place the roast in a roaster fat side up. Bake in a preheated 500° oven for 15 minutes until golden. Reduce the heat to 325°. Bake for 1 1/2 hours. Pour 3 tablespoons of the butter-chicken broth mixture over the roast every 15 minutes. Baste the meat with the pan juices when the basting mixture has run out. Serve hot with potatoes or rice. Serves 6 to 8.

Beef Roast
Pieczeń Wołowa

1 1/2 pounds prime beef
2 tablespoons oil
3 onions, sliced

salt and pepper to taste
1 bay leaf
1 pound mushrooms, optional

Brown the meat in hot oil on both sides. Add the onions, salt, pepper, and the bay leaf. Simmer, covered, for 1 1/2 hours. Add water to prevent burning. After an hour of simmering, add the mushrooms. Serve hot with boiled potatoes and salad. Serves 4 to 6.

Meat Loaf
Klops

1 pound ground beef
1 1/2 pounds ground pork
3 kaiser rolls, soaked in water
    and drained

2 fresh eggs
2 onions, chopped
salt and pepper
2 hard-cooked eggs, quartered

Blend the meat, drained wet rolls, fresh eggs and onion. Knead the mixture. Place half the mixture in a greased loaf pan. Place the hard-cooked egg quarters lengthwise and cover with the remaining meat. Press the meat into pan to prevent empty spots. Sprinkle with bread crumbs. Bake at 350° for 45 to 60 minutes. Serves 6.

Roast Duck with Apples
Kaczka z Jabłkami

1 duck
1 tablespoon salt
1/2 teaspoon marjoram

4 tart apples, sliced
2 tablespoons butter

Clean the duck well. Salt and set aside for 1 hour. Rub the inside of the duck with marjoram, then stuff with apples. Close the cavity and secure with toothpicks. Melt the butter in a baking pan and place the duck, breast up, in the pan. Bake at 450° for 45 minutes. Reduce heat to 350° and bake for another 30 minutes. When tender and golden, remove from the oven and cut into quarters. Arrange on a serving dish with the apples. Sprinkle with a little meat juice. Serve meat juices on the side. Serves 4.

Pork Cutlet
Kotlet Schabowy

4 pork chops
salt and pepper to taste
1 egg
1 teaspoon flour

2 tablespoons bread crumbs
2 tablespoons oil
1 teaspoon butter

Pound the pork chops until thin. Sprinkle with salt and pepper on both sides. Set aside for 1/2 hour. Whip the egg with a fork. Mix the flour with the bread crumbs. Dip each pork chop into the egg, and then the bread crumb mixture. Fry in hot oil until golden. Add the butter and a little water and cook covered for 10 minutes. Serve with boiled potatoes and sauerkraut.

Veal Roast
Pieczeń Cielęca

2 cloves garlic
1 1/2 pounds veal
2 tablespoons vegetable oil
1 tablespoon vegetable seasoning
   (a combination of dried onion,
   parsley and other vegetables,
   found at most markets)

1 tablespoon butter
salt and pepper
bay leaf

Cut the garlic into small pieces. With a sharp knife make holes in the meat and insert pieces of garlic. In a Dutch oven brown the veal in oil on both sides. Add the remaining ingredients and a little water and simmer for 1 hour, adding water frequently. Serve hot with boiled potatoes and salad, or as cold cuts. Serves 4.

Chicken in Aspic
Kurczak w Galarecie

Henryka Woźniak

1 big chicken, cleaned
1 carrot
1 stalk celery
2 parsley roots
1 leek
1 onion
1 bay leaf

salt and pepper to taste
1 envelope unflavored gelatin
1 cup green peas, cooked
2 hard-cooked eggs, optional
parsley, chopped
lemon juice

Place the chicken in a big pot, cover with water and bring to a boil. Skim off the foam. Add all the vegetables except the peas. Add spices. Cook until the chicken is tender. Set aside. When cool take the chicken and carrot out of the pot. Discard the skin and bones. Dice the meat. Slice the carrot. Strain off the bouillon, then skim off fat. Dissolve the gelatin in a little water. Stir into the bouillon; bring to a boil. In 4 individual serving dishes place halved hard-cooked eggs open face down. Divide the carrots, peas and chicken into each of the four serving dishes. Cover with bouillon. Refrigerate until set. Garnish with chopped parsley and sprinkle with lemon juice. Serves 4.

The Solidarity Tower at the Copernicus Cultural and Civic Center in Chicago, Illinois. This clock tower is modeled after the Warsaw Royal Castle in Poland.

153

Baked Saddle of Hare
Pieczony Comber Zajęczy

1 hare, cleaned (rabbit,
    optional)
1/2 pound pork fat, sliced

1 tablespoon butter
flour

Marinade:
1/2 pint red wine
1/2 pint beef stock
3 onions, sliced
1/2 teaspoon thyme

1 bay leaf
salt and pepper
juice of 1/2 lemon

Marinade: Boil all ingredients together and cool the mixture. Add the hare and refrigerate for 2 to 3 days. Remove the meat from the marinade, reserving the marinade. With a sharp knife make holes in the hare and stuff it with slices of pork fat. Bake in butter at 350°. Pour the marinade over the meat every few minutes. Bake until tender. Slice the hare and arrange on a serving platter; keep warm. To thicken the sauce, add flour to the pan drippings. Cook until bubbly. Add the marinade and cook to desired consistency. Serve the hare with sauce, noodles and vegetables. Serves 4.

Ryszarda Klim, her daughter Jolanta Drake, and two grandchildren display Polish folk art. Klim, a noted folk artist, and her family live in Milwaukee, Wisconsin.

Stuffed Peppers
Papryka Faszerowana

Henryka Woźniak

6 red peppers, cored
2 tablespoons plus 1 teaspoon
   butter or margarine, divided
1 carrot, sliced
1 parsley root, sliced
1 leek, sliced
2 stalks celery, sliced

2 onions, chopped
1 bay leaf
1/2 cup chicken broth
salt and pepper
3 tablespoons sour cream
1 teaspoon flour

Filling:

12 ounces ground pork
12 ounces ground beef
2 kaiser rolls, soaked in water

1 large onion, shredded
1 egg
salt and pepper

Combine all filling ingredients and mix well.

Fill each pepper with filling and place them into a greased casserole. Set aside. In 2 tablespoons butter over low heat sauté all the vegetables except the onions for 15 minutes. Put 1 teaspoon butter in a separate frying pan and sauté the onions until golden. Cover the prepared peppers with onion and vegetables. Add the bay leaf, broth, salt, and pepper. Cover casserole and simmer for 10 minutes. Blend the flour with sour cream and place 1 teaspoon of this on each pepper. Keep covered and simmer for another 10 minutes. Serves 6.

Kielbasa and Cabbage

Kowalski Sausage Company, Hamtramck, Michigan

A crockpot special. A regal feast made with popular dinner sausage.

1 small head cabbage,
  coarsely diced
1 onion, sliced
3 small potatoes, peeled and
  diced
1 teaspoon salt

1/2 teaspoon caraway seed
1 1/2 pounds kielbasa
  sausage, cut into 1-inch
  pieces
1 can (14 ounces) chicken
  broth

Put the vegetables, seasonings, and sausage in a crockpot. Pour in the chicken broth. Cover. Cook on low 6 to 10 hours, or on high 2 to 4 hours. Serves 4.

Elizabeth Zolna places rings of kielbasa on a truck for smoking at Kowalski Sausage Company.

Vegetables and Side Dishes

Matzo Knaidlach
(dumplings)
Knedle z Macy

Karyna Swistak,
College Park, Maryland

5 eggs, beaten
1 cup water
16 ounces matzo meal

1/4 cup salad oil
salt to taste

Combine the eggs, water and matzo meal. Add the oil and salt to taste. To cook dumplings, drop balls of dough into boiling salted water. Bring back to a boil and cook for 10 minutes. Remove with a slotted spoon. Serves 6.

Horseradish in Vinegar
Chrzan w Occie

5 horseradish roots
boiling water
1 cup white vinegar

salt
sugar

Clean and peel the horseradish; grate in a food processor or blender. Pour boiling water over the horseradish to get rid of the bitterness; drain. Add the vinegar. Add the salt and sugar to taste. Makes about 1 1/2 cups. Serve with meat, or add to salad dressings.

Stuffed Goose Necks
Nadziewane Szyjki Gęsie

Karyna Świstak

5 goose necks
2 pounds white potatoes
3 large onions, chopped
goose fat

3 eggs
salt and pepper to taste
sugar to taste

Draw the skin off the goose necks; scald, scrape and rinse them. Peel and grate the potatoes. Fry the onions in the goose fat until golden. Combine the fried onions, potatoes, eggs and seasonings. Stuff the necks with the potato mixture and sew up both ends. Simmer the necks 20 minutes in boiling salted water. Remove from water and place in a roaster greased with goose fat. Bake at 350° one hour. Serve as an appetizer or a buffet dish. Serves 4 to 6. Note: You may use bread or matzo instead of potatoes. Chicken or turkey necks may be used instead of goose necks. This dish is very popular.

Matzo Fritters
Placuszki z Macy

8 ounces matzos, broken
    into pieces
8 eggs, separated

salt and pepper to taste
oil for frying

Soak the matzo in boiling water for a few minutes and drain. Whip the egg whites into stiff peaks. Beat the egg yolks and add to the matzos. Fold in the egg whites, and salt and pepper to taste. Fry in hot oil. Serve as an accompaniment or as a main dish. Serves 8.

Egg Drops
Lane Kluski

Malgorzata Nowakowski

2 eggs, beaten
1/4 teaspoon salt
2 tablespoons milk

1/3 cup all-purpose flour
4 cups water or beef broth

Combine all the ingredients, except water or beef broth, in a large bowl and stir until smooth. Then bring 4 cups of water or broth to a boil. Pour and stir the prepared mixture into the boiling water. Cook about 2 minutes, until done. Serves 4.

Braised Beets

M. Nancy Stubeusz
Oneonta, New York

These beets are a delicious accompaniment to beef and game dishes.

2 pounds whole beets with about 1 inch of stem
2 cooking apples, peeled and grated
1 tablespoon dry red wine
3 tablespoons water

1 tablespoon minced onion
3 heaping tablespoons butter
2 tablespoons flour
salt
pinch sugar
lemon juice

Cook the beets until tender; drain, peel, and refrigerate overnight. Grate the beets coarsely and add the apples, red wine and water. Bring to a boil and simmer, covered, for 10 minutes. Meanwhile, sauté the onion in the butter until golden, then add flour. Stir until smooth and sauté until slightly browned. Add to the beet mixture. Season to taste with salt, sugar, and lemon juice. Simmer for a little longer. Serve hot. Serves 4.

Sauerkraut

2 pounds sauerkraut
6 slices smoked bacon
2 tablespoons bacon fat
1 carrot, sliced
1 large onion, sliced
salt and black pepper
4 juniper berries, crushed,
   optional

1 tablespoon caraway seed
2 cups white wine
1 1/2 cups chicken stock or
   water
1 garlic sausage
4 to 6 frankfurters

Put the drained sauerkraut into a colander and steep in cold water for 20 minutes, changing the water twice. Drain and squeeze dry, then unravel the strands of cabbage as much as possible. Preheat oven to 300°. Cut the smoked bacon into strips 2 inches long. Melt the fat in a flame-proof casserole and then fry the bacon, carrot, and onion lightly without browning. Stir in the sauerkraut, and generous seasoning of black pepper, and salt. Add the juniper berries, if used, caraway seed, wine, and stock or water. Bring to a simmering point; cover tightly and transfer to center of oven. Cook for 3 hours, then push the garlic sausage into center of the sauerkraut. Continue cooking another 1 to 1 1/2 hours. Add the frankfurters 20 minutes before serving. Check seasoning and serve. Serves 4 to 6.

Father Cornelian Dende, director of the Father Justin Rosary Hour for thirty-six years, and Daniel Kij, former president Polish Union of America, in Radio Center in Athol Springs, New York. The woodcarving of Our Lady of the Divine Word is by the late Jan Mentel of Montreal, Canada.

Baked Mushrooms
Pieczarki Nadziewane

Malgorzata Nowakowski

Christmas Eve dish.

1 pound mushrooms	1/2 cup bread crumbs
2 onions, chopped	1/2 cup sour cream
3 tablespoons butter or	1/2 cup chopped parsley
margarine	salt and pepper to taste

Clean the mushrooms, removing the stems. Arrange the mushrooms, heads down, on a greased pan. Preheat oven to 375°. Chop the mushroom stems; set aside. Lightly brown the onions in the butter. Add the mushroom stems and cook for 3 minutes. Stir in the bread crumbs and sour cream. Mix well. Add the parsley, salt, and pepper. Cook for another minute. Fill each mushroom cap with the stuffing. Bake for 15 minutes. Serves 4.

Beet Purée
Buraczki Gotowane

Malgorzata Nowakowski

6 medium-sized cooked beets, peeled	2 tablespoons lemon juice
3 tablespoons butter	1 teaspoon salt
1 tablespoon flour, dissolved in 1/4 cup water	1 tablespoon sugar
	1 tablespoon sour cream

Grate the beets into a pan and, stirring constantly, add all the ingredients except the sour cream. Cover and simmer for about 10 minutes. Stir in the sour cream. Serve hot. Serves 4.

Noodles with Poppy Seed
Kluski z Makiem

Christmas Eve Dish.

4 cups all-purpose flour	1 tablespoon cream cheese
1 egg, beaten	1 cup poppy seeds, crushed
1/2 teaspoon salt	1 tablespoon sugar
1 tablespoon butter	2 tablespoons butter

Place the flour in a large bowl or on smooth working surface. Make a well in the flour and pour the egg and salt into the well; mix in. Cream the butter and cream cheese and add to dough. Work the dough with a knife, then with your hands, adding water to form a dough that is stiff and not sticky. Roll the dough out thin and cut it into 1-inch strips. Sprinkle each strip with flour. Pile the strips and cut into even thinner strips. The dough should not stick if it is of the right consistency. Put the raw noodles on a board. Separate them with your fingers and allow them to dry for a while. To cook, place in boiling salted water and boil for 2 to 5 minutes. Drain the noodles and place in a deep dish. Sprinkle with poppy seeds and sugar. In a small frying pan, heat butter until golden brown. Sprinkle the noodles with golden brown butter. Honey may be used in place of sugar. Serves 4.

Dill Pickles
Ogórki Kiszone

1 quart water	10 stalks fresh dill weed
2 tablespoons salt	5 cloves garlic
2 pounds pickling cucumbers	2 inches horseradish root

Boil the water and salt. Let cool. Arrange the cucumbers in a stoneware jar. Add the dill, garlic, and horseradish root. Add the salted water. Cover with an upside-down plate and a weight on the plate. Set aside for 4 to 5 days in the summer or 7 to 8 days in the winter. Makes 2 pounds.

Potato Pancakes
Placki Ziemniaczane

Adela Zydel
Worcester, New York

This is a family recipe, guaranteed to excite the palate.

1 to 2 onions, chopped fine	2 to 3 eggs
4 tablespoons butter, divided	2 to 3 tablespoons flour
5 medium-sized potatoes	1 teaspoon salt

Fry the onions in 1 tablespoon butter until browned. Grate the potatoes into a medium-sized bowl. Melt 1 tablespoon of butter. Add the melted butter, onions, eggs, flour and salt to the potatoes; mix well. Place 1 tablespoon of the remaining butter into a large frying pan. When the pan is hot and the butter is melted, drop spoonfuls of the potato mixture into the hot pan and fry until golden brown. Turn the pancakes over and fry the other side. Add remaining butter as needed. Makes 15 pancakes. Can be refrigerated or frozen and used later. Serves 4 to 6.

Lenten Compote
Kompot Wigilijny

Christmas Eve Dinner

2 quarts water	5 ounces dried apricots
8 ounces dried pitted prunes	3 dried figs
5 ounces dried apples	juice of 1/2 lemon
5 ounces dried pears	sugar

Combine the water and the dried fruit. Bring to a boil, reduce heat and simmer over low heat for 10 to 15 minutes. Add the lemon juice and sugar to taste. Prepare at least 3 hours before serving. Serve cool. Serves 6.

Simmered Mushrooms
Grzyby Duszone

Henryka Woźniak

1 pound mushrooms
2 teaspoons butter
2 large yellow onions,
   chopped
small carrot, chopped,
   optional

1/4 cup chopped parsley,
   optional
salt and pepper to taste
3 tablespoons sour cream
1 teaspoon flour

Clean and thinly slice the mushrooms. Place into a pot of boiling water for a few seconds and drain. Melt the butter in a medium-sized pan. Add the mushrooms, onions, carrot, and parsley. Add salt and pepper and simmer for one hour, adding water if needed. Combine the sour cream and flour. Reduce heat and pour the sour cream mixture over the mushroom mixture. Simmer for 15 minutes and add additional salt and pepper to taste. Serve with boiled potatoes or boiled buckwheat, carrot and apple. Serves 4.

Left to Right: Edith Ann Malson, Joyce Banchowski, Rita Michalak and Jeannette Wianecki, in Polish costumes, are shown at the Holiday Folk Fair, Milwaukee, Wisconsin, holding art work from Poland. They belong to the Polanki *Club of the Polish Women's Cultural Club.*

Beets with Horseradish
Ćwikła

This dish is typically served at Easter.

2 horseradish roots
3 small beets
1 teaspoon salt

2 teaspoons sugar
juice of 1 lemon
1/2 cup boiling water

Soak the horseradish in water for 6 hours. Then peel the roots. Finely grate the roots and sprinkle them with salt to prevent darkening. Set aside. Boil the beets for 30 minutes, cool, then peel them. Grate the beets. Scald the horseradish, drain and cool. Combine the salt, sugar, and lemon juice together with the water. Add to the horseradish. Add the grated beets and mix well. Put into a jar. Keep in the refrigerator. Serve as a side dish. Serves 4.

Pea Purée
Purée z Groszku

1 pound fresh or frozen peas
4 cloves of garlic, divided
1 teaspoon dried rosemary

1 teaspoon butter
1 small onion, chopped
salt and pepper to taste

Pour enough water to cover peas into a pan; add 3 cloves garlic, rosemary, and salt (but not the peas). Bring to a boil. Boil for 15 to 20 minutes. Add peas and continue to boil for another 5 minutes. Remove garlic from peas and place the undrained pea mixture into a blender or food processor. Purée and set aside. Sauté the onion and remaining garlic in butter until golden. Add to peas. Season to taste. Serves 4.

Noodles with
Poppyseed and Raisins
Kluski z Makiem i Rodzynkami

Virginia Luty

2 cups egg noodles, cooked
2 tablespoons melted butter
1 can (12 ounces) poppy seed
   cake and pastry filling
1 teaspoon vanilla extract

1 teaspoon lemon juice
1 1/2 teaspoons grated lemon
   rind
1/3 cup raisins

Toss the cooked noodles with melted butter. Combine the poppyseed filling with vanilla, lemon juice, lemon rind, and raisins. Add the noodles and mix well. Serve warm. Serves 6.

Spinach
Szpinak

2 pounds fresh spinach,
   cleaned
1/2 cup water
1 tablespoon butter
1 tablespoon flour

1 tablespoon sour cream
1 clove garlic, crushed
1 egg, beaten
salt and pepper to taste

Simmer the spinach in water over very low heat for 10 minutes. Place the spinach in a very fine sieve and rinse with cold water. Chop the spinach in a blender, place in a pan and set aside. In a small pan melt the butter and sprinkle with flour; stir until smooth. Stir into spinach. Add the sour cream, garlic, egg, salt, and pepper. Mix well. Heat mixture, stirring constantly. Good on its own or as a side dish. Serves 2 to 4.

Desserts

Cheese Dessert
Deser z Sera

Lila Lam-Nowakowska

Dessert:

1 package vanilla pudding mix
1/2 cup milk
2 8-ounce packages cream
  cheese
2 eggs
1 cup sugar

1 teaspoon vanilla extract
1/2 cup raisins
1/2 cup chopped walnuts
12 to 15 *petits beurres* (French
  butter cookies)

Chocolate Frosting:

1 tablespoon butter
1 tablespoon cocoa

1 tablespoon sugar

Dessert: Blend the pudding mix with the milk until smooth. Set aside. Combine the cream cheese, eggs, sugar and vanilla extract in a double boiler over hot water. Cook and stir until smooth. Do not let boil. Add the pudding mixture and continue to cook over hot water until the mixture becomes thick, stirring constantly. Add the raisins and walnuts. In a tart pan place half of the *petits beurres* along the bottom and pour the cheese mixture over top. Place the remaining *petits beurres* over the still hot mixture and set aside to cool.

Chocolate Frosting: Combine all the ingredients in a pan and bring to a boil over low heat. Pour the mixture over the cool dessert. Refrigerate and serve cold. Serves 4 to 6.

Cheese Blintzes
Naleśniki z Serem

Lila Lam-Nowakowska

Batter:

1 egg
1 cup flour
1 cup skim milk

1 teaspoon oil
salt to taste
oil for frying

Filling:

1 pound cream cheese
2 eggs
vanilla sugar to taste

raisins
grated lemon peel

Batter: Blend all the ingredients together. The batter should have consistency similar to buttermilk. If too thick, add milk. Cover the bottom of a frying pan with a thin layer of oil and heat over medium-high heat. Pour some batter evenly over the pan to form a thin pancake. Fry on both sides and then set aside, on an upside-down plate. Let cool. Repeat for more pancakes.

Filling: Blend the cheese with the rest of ingredients. Don't make it too sweet. Fill each pancake with the cheese mixture, spreading it evenly on the surface of the blintz. Fold it in four or roll it, folding the edges inside. Cook in the same skillet until browned on both sides. Serves 4.

Note: Different fillings can be used. Meat, cabbage, mushroom, or fruit preserves are good. It is a custom to fold the blintzes with sweet filling and roll the meat-filled blintzes.

Polish silver in the Polish Museum of America, Chicago, Illinois.

Pear Compote
Kompot z Gruszek

Malgorzata Nowakowski

4 pears
3/4 cup white wine
1/3 cup sugar
2 tablespoons red currant jelly

2 tablespoons lemon juice
4 cloves
whipped cream

Pare the pears, leaving whole with stems attached. Combine all the remaining ingredients except the whipped cream and bring to boiling. Add the pears and simmer until they are transparent on the edges, about forty minutes. Remove the pears from the syrup and place them in a serving dish. Boil the syrup until very thick. Pour over the pears. Chill. Serve with the whipped cream.

Plum Cake
Ciasto ze Śliwkami

Lila Lam-Nowakowska

1/2 cup butter or margarine
1 cup granulated sugar
2 eggs
2 cups all-purpose flour
2 teaspoons baking powder
salt
3/4 cup milk

40 fresh plums (damson or
    Italian), pitted and cut in
    half, or 2 cans (30-ounce)
    whole purple plums,
    drained and pitted
3 tablespoons butter
1/4 cup ground cloves

In a food processor beat the butter together with the sugar. Add the eggs and process for 2 minutes. Combine the flour, baking powder, and salt; add to the sugar mixture, then gradually add the milk while mixing constantly on a low speed. Grease and flour a 9x13-inch baking pan. Pour prepared dough in pan. Place plums on the top. Dot with butter and sprinkle with cloves. Bake at 350° for about 40 minutes.

Sweet Crisps
Chruściki

Mary K. Gorecka
Pennington, New Jersey

6 egg yolks
2 teaspoons salt
1 cup sugar
4 ounces butter, softened
1 teaspoon vanilla
2 tablespoons whisky

1 teaspoon baking soda
7 cups sifted flour
1 pint sour cream
shortening for deep frying
powdered sugar

Beat the egg yolks and salt for 10 minutes. Gradually add the sugar. Beat in the butter, vanilla, whisky, and baking soda. Alternately add the flour and sour cream. Mix well. Roll out thin, then cut into rectangles 1 1/2x4 inches. Cut a slit down the center of each rectangle and weave one end through. Deep fry the cookies about 6 at a time in hot shortening (about 350°) until golden. Drain on paper towels, cool and dust with powdered sugar before serving.

Apricot Fool
Kisiel Morelowy

Malgorzata Nowakowski

1 pound fresh or canned
   apricots
1/2 cup sugar

3 cups water, divided
3 tablespoons potato starch
whipped cream

Clean and halve the apricots. Combine them with sugar and 2 cups water. Bring to boiling, then simmer for 10 minutes until the apricots are tender. Then blend until the mixture becomes smooth. Put aside. Blend the remaining water with the potato starch. Pour little by little into the fruit mixture, stirring constantly. Bring to boiling over very low heat. Serve in separate bowls with whipped cream on top. Serves 4.

Gingerbread
Piernik

In Polish slang Piernik *means an old person. With gingerbread, older is better.*

1/2 teaspoon cinnamon
1/2 teaspoon ground cloves
1/2 teaspoon nutmeg
1/4 teaspoon ginger
1/4 teaspoon black pepper
1/4 teaspoon baking powder
1 teaspoon baking soda
1 1/2 cups flour
1 1/2 cups rye flour
1 1/2 cups sugar

1/2 cup butter
1 cup honey
3 eggs, separated
1/2 cup kefir or buttermilk
1/2 cup sour cream
prunes, chopped, optional
figs, chopped, optional
raisins, optional
bread crumbs

Sift together the spices, baking powder, baking soda, and flours. In a separate bowl cream the butter and sugar; add the honey and egg yolks. Add the butter mixture to the flour mixture. Add the kefir and sour cream, mix well. Beat the egg whites until stiff, then fold into dough. If you use the dried fruit, coat it with flour to prevent it from sinking; fold in. Grease a deep baking dish and sprinkle with bread crumbs. Pour the dough into baking dish and bake at 350° for 1 hour.

Note: Should be made ahead of time for a better taste.

Street scene in Poland

—Drawing by Alice Wadowski-Bak

Quick Yeast Cake
Ciasto Drożdżowe

Lila Lam-Nowakowska

"This is my mother's recipe. She calls this a quick bread even though it takes two days. All you do for this is wait."

—*Jacek Nowakowski*

2 ounces fresh yeast
1/2 cup warm water
2 cups granulated sugar
3/4 cup milk
1 cup margarine or butter

4 eggs
1 teaspoon vanilla extract
salt
4 cups all-purpose flour

Dissolve the yeast in 1/2 cup warm water. Combine all the other ingredients except the flour and beat well until mixed. Stir in the yeast. Let it rise at room temperature overnight, 10 hours. Stir in the flour gradually. Add enough flour to make a stiff dough. Set aside for another six hours. Form the dough to fit a greased bread pan and let rise for another 1 to 2 hours. Bake at 350° for about 45 minutes or until golden.

Looking at a Szopka, Christmas crèche, are Irena Franuszkiewicz, who founded the Christmas Reflections program; Khrista Kowalski, Darlene Jurek, and Ross Olinski at the Polish Museum of America, Chicago.

Cheesecake
Serowiec or Sernik

Malgorzata Nowakowski

1/2 cup raisins	3 packages (8-ounce) cream
3 tablespoons flour, divided	cheese, softened
1/4 teaspoon salt	1 cup sugar
5 eggs, separated	1 tablespoon grated lemon peel

Soak the raisins in hot water for 15 minutes. Pat dry and coat with 2 tablespoons of flour. Set aside. Preheat the oven to 350°. Beat the egg whites and salt until stiff. Place the egg white mixture in the freezer for 5 minutes. Combine the cheese, sugar, egg yolks, and remaining flour; beat until smooth. Stir in the raisins and lemon peel. Carefully fold in the egg whites. Pour the mixture into a greased and floured 9-inch springform pan. Bake for 45 minutes, then turn the oven off and leave the cake in the oven until it cools.

Fruitcake
Keks or Cwibak

Two names in Polish are common for the same cake. The name varies with the region you are in.

1/2 pound sugar	3/4 cup candied orange peel,
1 cup butter or margarine	chopped
5 eggs	2/3 cup raisins
2 cups flour	2/3 cup walnuts, finely
1 shot glass of vodka or other	chopped
grain alcohol	1/2 cup sliced dried figs
2 teaspoons baking powder	1/2 cup pitted dried prunes,
1 teaspoon vanilla	diced

Cream the sugar and butter, add the eggs, flour, alcohol, baking powder, and vanilla. Blend until smooth. Toss the fruit and nuts with enough flour to coat. Add to the batter. Place the batter in an 11x7x3-inch greased and floured loaf pan. Bake at 350° for 1 hour.

Honey Almond Cookies
Pierniczki z Migdałami

1 cup honey
3 eggs
3 cups sifted flour
1 teaspoon baking soda
1/2 teaspoon nutmeg

1/2 teaspoon ginger
1 teaspoon cinnamon
2 egg whites, slightly beaten
blanched almond halves

Beat together the honey and eggs. Add the flour, baking soda, and spices; mix well. Shape the mixture into a ball and refrigerate for several hours. Roll the dough out on a floured surface to 1/2-inch thick and cut with a round cookie cutter. Place the cookies on a greased baking sheet. Brush cookies with the egg whites and press an almond half into each. Bake at 350° for about 15 minutes.

Sandwich Cookies
with Jam
Chopins

Paula Marek
Greendale, Wisconsin

1 cup butter, softened
1/2 cup sugar
2 cups flour

1 cup finely ground walnuts
jam of your choice
powdered sugar

Blend the butter, sugar, flour, and nuts. Roll out on a lightly floured board to about 1/4 inch thick. Cut into circles, using a cookie cutter. Bake on ungreased cookie sheets for about 10 minutes at 350°. Remove from oven. Spread jam on half of the cookies while still warm and top with remaining cookies to form a sandwich. Sprinkle with powdered sugar if desired.

Holding honey ginger cookies at the Christmas Reflections program of the Polish Museum of America in Chicago, Illinois, are Wanda Kass and Carole Norris of Chicago and Rita Rose Rejewski Mauermann of Milwaukee, Wisconsin.

Shortcake
Kruche Ciasto

4 cups flour
1/2 cup powdered sugar or granulated sugar
1 cup cold butter or margarine
2 egg yolks

1 packet (5/16-ounce) vanilla sugar
2 tablespoons sour cream
1 teaspoon lemon juice
grated lemon rind
pinch salt

Combine the flour and sugar. Cut in the butter with a knife or pastry blender. Add the remaining ingredients. Knead the dough quickly to prevent it from warming. Wrap in foil or plastic wrap and refrigerate for 2 to 3 hours. Roll out the dough and cut into the desired cake shapes. It may be used for cookies or shortcakes. Bake at 350° for 30 minutes.

"Sand" Baba
Babka Piaskowa

1/2 cup butter
1/2 cup sugar
4 eggs
1/2 cup milk

vanilla extract
1 cup flour
1 teaspoon baking soda
1 teaspoon lemon juice

Preheat the oven to 350°. Cream the butter and sugar together. Add the eggs, beating after each one. Add the milk, and vanilla extract to taste. Add the flour and beat. Blend in the soda and lemon juice and pour into a greased loaf pan. Place in the hot oven immediately after adding the soda and lemon juice, or the cake will not rise. Bake for 45 minutes.

Kefir Cake
Ciasto Kefirowe

1 1/2 cups kefir or buttermilk
3 cups sugar
3 cups flour
6 eggs

2 tablespoons baking powder
2 packets (5/16-ounces)
   vanilla sugar
1 1/2 cups vegetable oil

Combine all the ingredients except the oil, and mix. Add the vegetable oil and mix well. Put into a 9x13-inch square baking pan. Bake for 50 minutes at 350°.

Easter Baba
Babka Wielkanocna

1 1/2 ounces yeast
1 tablespoon warm milk
1/2 cup sugar, divided
4 cups flour, divided
3 egg yolks
vanilla sugar to taste

grated lemon rind
pinch of salt
1 cup milk
1/3 cup butter, melted
1/2 cup raisins
bread crumbs

Dissolve the yeast in warm milk; add a teaspoon of sugar and 1 teaspoon of flour. In another bowl, beat the egg yolks with the rest of the sugar until light. Put the remaining flour into a large bowl. Make a well in the flour. Pour the yeast mixture into well; cover with flour. Wait for the yeast to grow. If it doesn't, add more yeast. Add the egg yolk mixture, vanilla sugar, lemon rind, and salt, mix well. Add the milk gradually. Knead the dough for about 5 minutes and add the melted butter, blending it through the dough. Toss the raisins with enough flour to coat and add to dough. Grease a 12-inch fluted pan or turban mold; sprinkle with bread crumbs. Pour batter into pan. Cover and let rise for 1 hour. Bake at 350° for 1 hour.

Walnut Horns
Rogaliki Orzechowe

Lila Lam-Nowakowska

1/3 cup granulated sugar	1 1/2 cups flour
2/3 cup ground walnuts	1/2 cup powdered sugar
1/3 cup butter or margarine	

Combine all the ingredients except the powdered sugar and mix until smooth. Put the dough into freezer for about 30 minutes. Roll 1 tablespoon of dough in your hands, place on a greased baking sheet and shape into a horn or crescent. Repeat with remaining dough. Bake at 350° for 10 to 15 minutes. While cookies are still warm, coat with powdered sugar. Makes about 3 dozen.

Mazurek

1/3 pound butter	5 ounces almonds, peeled,
4 hard-cooked egg yolks,	ground
mashed	salt
1 raw egg yolk	1 1/3 cups flour
5 ounces sugar	1 egg, beaten
grated lemon rind	preserves

Cream the butter in a large bowl. Add the hard-cooked egg yolks, egg yolk, sugar, lemon rind, almonds, salt, and flour. Mix well. Knead the dough for about 5 to 10 minutes. Place the dough in freezer for 1 hour. Roll 2/3 of the dough into an 8 1/2x11-inch rectangle. Take the remaining dough and roll it into strips the width of a pencil. Take the strips and place horizontally and vertically across the rectangle to form many squares. Brush the dough with the beaten egg and bake at 350° for 40 minutes. Cool and put the preserves or *povidla* in each square.

Note: A different cake can be made with the same (Mazurek) dough. This is Mazurka, a layer cake. For this, make three to four layers and fill each layer with preserves, peanut butter, chocolate or dried fruits. Frost the top.

Polish Poppyseed Roll
Makowiec

Genie O'Shesky
Dearborn, Michigan

5 to 6 cups all-purpose flour, divided
2 packages active dry yeast
1 1/2 cups milk

1/3 cup sugar
1/3 cup shortening
1 teaspoon salt
3 eggs

Poppyseed Filling:
1 cup boiling water
3/4 cup poppyseeds
1 cup lukewarm water
1/2 cup chopped nuts

1/3 cup honey
1 teaspoon grated lemon peel
1 egg white, stiffly beaten

In a large mixer bowl combine 2 cups flour and the yeast. Heat the milk, sugar, shortening, and salt till warm (115° to 120°), stirring constantly to melt shortening. Add to the dry mixture; add the eggs. Beat at low speed with electric mixer for 1/2 minutes, scraping bowl. Beat 3 minutes at high speed. By hand, stir in enough remaining flour to make a moderately stiff dough. Turn out on floured surface and knead till smooth and elastic (5 to 10 minutes). Shape into a ball. Place in greased bowl; turn once. Cover; let rise in warm place till doubled (1 to 1 3/4 hours). Punch the dough down; divide in half. Cover; let rest 10 minutes. On floured surface, roll each half to 24x8-inch rectangle; spread each with half the Poppyseed Filling. Roll up, starting at short end; seal long ends. Place, seam side down, in greased 9x5x3-inch loaf pans. Cover; let rise till double (30 to 45 minutes). Bake at 350° for 35 to 40 minutes. Remove from pans; cool. Makes 2 loaves.

Poppyseed Filling: Pour the boiling water over the poppyseeds; drain. Cover with the lukewarm water and let stand 30 minutes. Drain thoroughly. Grind the poppyseeds in blender or use the finest blade of food grinder. Stir in the chopped nuts, honey, and grated lemon peel. Fold in the stiffly beaten egg white.

Polish Cookies

Malgorzata Nowakowski

2 cups all-purpose flour	1 cup powdered sugar
1 cup butter or margarine	strawberries, halved
3 hard-cooked egg yolks	

Cream:

3/4 cup butter	1 whole egg
1 1/2 cups powdered sugar	1 egg yolk
	3 teaspoons cocoa

Dough: Combine all ingredients except strawberries and blend with a knife until crumbly. Mix with hands until dough is stiff. Form into a ball. Cover with plastic wrap and refrigerate 30 minutes. Roll out on a floured surface to about 1/4 inch thick. Cut into 1 1/2-inch rounds or other shapes. Place on greased cookie sheets. Bake at 375° for 10 to 12 minutes or until cookies are golden. **Cream:** Beat butter and sugar until fluffy. Add egg and yolk and beat until well-mixed. Beat in the cocoa. Put a teaspoon of the cream on the top of each cookie. Garnish with strawberry halves.

Enjoying jelly doughnuts are members of the Syrena Dance Ensemble, P.R.C.U.A., of Dearborn Heights, Michigan.

Filled Doughnuts
Pączki

3 packages active dry yeast
1/2 cup lukewarm milk
6 cups flour
1 cup milk, scalded and
    cooled
2 teaspoons salt
20 egg yolks
3/4 cup sugar

1 1/2 ounces rum
1 cup melted butter
cherry jam, use jam
    sweetened only with fruit
    juice if available
oil for deep frying
powdered sugar for
    sprinkling

Dissolve the yeast in the lukewarm milk for 5 minutes. Sift the flour into the scalded milk gradually. Add the yeast mixture, stirring until smooth. Let rise for 1/2 hour. Beat the salt into the egg yolks; add to flour mixture, mix well. Add the sugar and rum. Mix well. Knead until the dough no longer sticks to the sides. Gradually knead in the butter. Place in a greased bowl, turn to coat and let rise until doubled. Punch down and let rise again. Cut the dough in half, set one half aside and roll out the second half about 1/4 inch thick. Using a 2-inch biscuit cutter cut as many rounds as possible. Place a dab of cherry jam on one round, cover jam with another round and seal edges. Place the filled doughnuts on greased sheets, allowing room between each for rising. Repeat the process until all the dough is used. Let the doughnuts rise for about 1 hour or until doubled. Pour the oil into deep fryer or deep pan (about 5 inches). Heat the oil until it is about 360 to 370°. Deep fry the doughnuts in oil for about 3 minutes per side or until golden brown on both sides.

Wycinanki *by Alice Wadowski-Bak.*

1988 photograph

Chicago has approximately 40 blocks of Polish-American businesses serving new immigrants from Poland, older immigrants, and second- and third-generation descendants. More than 100,000 Polish immigrants came to Chicago in the 1980s.

Ben Schultz, volunteer at the Polish Musem, Winona, Minnesota, holds the prayer books of the immigrants. Background photo shows the Polish Legion Band playing cards in 1910 in Winona.

Sites of Interest to Polish Americans

Illinois: Polish Museum of America, sponsored by the Polish Roman Catholic Union of America, Chicago; Polka Music Hall of Fame, sponsored by the International Polka Association, Chicago.

Indiana: Shrines of the Discalced Carmelites, Munster.

Michigan: Orchard Lake Schools, Orchard Lake.

Minnesota : Polish Museum, Winona.

Missouri: Black Madonna Shrine and Grottos, Eureka.

New York: St. Francis High School Faculty House, Athol Springs, featuring murals depicting historic Polish events.

Pennsylvania: National Shrine of Our Lady of Częstochowa, Doylestown; Polish Room, University of Pittsburgh, Pittsburgh.

Texas: Oldest Polish settlement in America, Panna Maria. Other Polish settlements in San Antonio, Yorktown, Bandera, Saint Hedwig, Częstochowa, Kościuszko, Falls City, Polonia, and Pawelekville.

Washington, D.C.: Mary Queen of Poland Chapel, National Shrine of the Immaculate Conception; busts of Tadeusz Kościuszko and Kazimierz Pułaski sculpted by Polish-American sculptor Henryk Dmochowski, Capitol rotunda.